Jonie
Goes To College

How can the fleeting years of college with all their fun,
hard work, and spiritual benefits be packed into so few
pages? I can only begin to share my own experience,
hoping that those who yet look forward to college will
realize that it is one of the most important periods of life
and will, therefore, strive to gain the most from those
precious years. And perhaps those who have not the
desire to continue their education will realize something of what they are missing and, perhaps, change
their minds.

—Jonie

Jonie

Goes To College

Jo-An Ritchie

Review and Herald Publishing Association
Washington, D.C. 20012

Copyright © 1982 by the
Review and Herald Publishing Association
Washington, D.C. 20012

This book was
edited by Bobbie Jane Van Dolson
Cover illustration by Gary R. Huff

Type set: 10/11 Century Schoolbook

Printed in U.S.A.

Library of Congress Card No. 81-86082
ISBN 0-8280-0116-2

Contents

Dedication

Dedicated
to Norman Henderson,
who challenged my faith;
to Harry Thomsen,
for the patient hours of kindly coaching;
to Don Winger,
whose high principles and Christian example
were a daily inspiration;
and to all my dormitory sisters in old West Hall,
who helped make the memories.

A Change of Scenery

THE PIGEONS picking up crumbs took flight and settled on the telephone wire. They cooed a soft warning as Jonie Owens' shadow darkened the sidewalk ahead of her. It was one of those sunny, brisk, glad-to-be-alive mornings. The slim, dark-haired girl sniffed appreciatively at the warm, yeasty odor of baking bread as she hurried toward the white building where several equally white trucks were being filled with bakery goods. Three or four young men, busily carrying large boxes of bread and trays of pies, cakes, and other pastries, nodded and smiled as she hurried inside to put on a uniform and a long white apron.

The room-sized butcher-block table was surrounded by white-capped men who were rolling out dough on the floured surface. Jonie turned toward her own corner and counted thirty-six cakes waiting to be frosted and decorated. Not a bad morning, she thought, as she read the orders, then began measuring out the powdered sugar for frosting.

Today's payday. I hope we get finished up early enough to get to the bank before it closes, she mused. She turned on the mixer, and the heavy, three-foot blades lightly scraped the side of the four-foot cylinder-shaped tub. The creamy white mixture within began to take on a fluffy appearance, and Jonie turned the speed up a bit. "Oh, dear, I can't remember whether I put the vanilla in!" With a swipe of her little finger across the inside of the tub Jonie gathered a bit of frosting, but she was not quick enough to miss contact with the giant blade. The errant finger was badly pinched and turned blue within a few minutes. By noon the throbbing was considerably worse and the nail was black.

At lunch one of the women who worked in the bakery called to Jonie to come and eat with her, but Jonie shook her head. Mrs. Stonner noted the pained look on the usually smiling features and came over to where the sufferer sat alone. "You look a little pale. Don't you feel well, Jonie?" she asked sympathetically.

"It's just my finger," Jonie answered. "I did something foolish."

The woman lifted the discolored hand and gently examined the bruised digit. "What on earth, child?" she exclaimed. "Why didn't you say anything? Let me run you over to the clinic."

Fifteen minutes later Jonie sat in the doctor's office watching a bit apprehensively as he heated a wire redhot over an open flame. He held her finger in the light and touched the wire to the black nail. *Sssst!* A small hole appeared, followed instantly by a tiny spurt of blood, which gave Jonie immediate relief from the pressure that had been building in the injured finger all morning.

The girl looked up with gratitude, a smile once again lighting her pretty face.

"Better, huh?" the doctor said.

"Oh, so much! And you did it so quickly! Now I can frost the rest of the cakes, and I don't think it will get in my way at all. It hardly hurts," she said happily as he wrapped the finger and put a guard over it. "Thanks a million."

He laughed at her enthusiasm. "Most people would use this as a good excuse to take the rest of the day off."

"Not me. I've got to get in all the time I can if I'm going to college this fall."

"Good for you!" he said, and cautioned her to come back if the finger gave her any trouble.

Back at the bakery, Jonie continued where she had left off. There were cinnamon buns to be iced and nutty bear claws to be boxed. The day passed rapidly, and after checking out, Jonie hurried to the bank to deposit her paycheck.

Now, if I'm very careful I should have more than enough for the entrance fee this fall, Jonie thought as she hurried for the bus that would take her home. She had allowed herself enough cash to last until the following payday and her tithe check was already written and tucked in her purse to be deposited in the church offering plate the following day.

Jonie usually spent Sabbath with her close friend Chuck Richards and his family. Arriving home, she hurried into the house to prepare something to contribute to the Sabbath dinner, which was often eaten outdoors. Mrs. Owens greeted her warmly and pointed to a cake waiting to be frosted. Mother and daughter were soon busily engaged with frosting and laughter. "You'd think I could find something better to do after working in a bakery all day," Jonie stated. "And, by the way, I agreed to go over after sundown Saturday night and get some orders ready for Sunday."

"I hope you won't be too late," her mother replied with concern. "Sundown is so late these summer days, and I dislike having you down there alone."

"Oh, I'll be all right, Mother," Jonie said, licking a spoon.

"Well, it's not exactly the best part of town to be walking in at night. I wish your father and I weren't going to be gone this weekend. I just don't like the idea one bit." Donna Owens was becoming more disturbed.

"But, Mother, I have to finish things up Saturday night. That was part of the job agreement since I don't work Sabbath. And I'll be careful. Besides, I *do* have a guardian angel."

"Yes, Jonie, but you have a way of working him overtime."

"Not purposely, Mother," Jonie said seriously. "Maybe Chuck could use his dad's car and come to get me." Mrs. Owens nodded. Her concern was not unwarranted, and she breathed a silent prayer for Jonie's safety.

Sabbath was hot, and Chuck and Jonie and his family welcomed the drive up the Columbia River gorge. They ate lunch at a park along the way and then continued on to Multnomah Falls. Glancing back at grand old Mount Hood, Jonie remarked about the melting snow level on the lofty peaks. "Someday I want to climb to the top of that mountain."

"Well, today we'll climb to the top of the falls," Chuck told her.

"How long does it take?"

"Not very long," he said, putting an arm around Jonie. She smiled up at him just as Mr. Richards glanced in the rear-view mirror and saw the expression of love on his son's face.

"You know, I have to agree with King Solomon," the man said.

"How is that?" Jonie asked.

"Well, as wise as he was, he said there were four things he couldn't understand—the bird on the wing, the serpent crawling on a rock, the ship finding its way on the sea, and the way of a man with a maid. In other words, the growth of love."

There was silence in the back seat. Chuck was certain that a lecture was about to be delivered.

"Love never stands still. It must either go forward or backward," continued Mr. Richards. "I think we should consider where it leads as it grows. You two have been close friends since grade school, and as you neared the end of your senior year in academy it became obvious that you were interested in no one else, but preferred a steady relationship with each other. True?"

"That's true," Jonie replied, looking up at Chuck. The pressure of his arm about her shoulder tightened slightly as he looked seriously out the window.

"Now, if love doesn't stand still, in most instances, it will eventually lead to marriage. But, in your situation, you both have a strong desire to finish college."

"And we are very proud of you both," Mrs. Richards added quickly.

"Yes, we are proud, but concerned. It is another four years until graduation, and four years is a long time to continue a serious romance. No one needs to tell two 18-year-olds about the birds and the bees. You are well aware of the explosive material love is made of. Two people start out holding hands; they kiss, and if love keeps growing, and the two lovers choose to obey God's rule for happiness it becomes a constant battle to refrain from the acts of marriage. I think this deserves prayerful consideration. And please do not take this personally, Jonie. We love you very much, and nothing could make us happier than to have you as part of the family someday, should you and Chuck become so committed. But for now college is a time for getting to know oneself, choosing a career, making many friends and, most important, letting God help you choose a mate. Only He knows what is really right for your future happiness."

Chuck's little sister, riding between her parents in the front seat, began to squirm. Her mother smiled down at her. "You may not be quite 12 yet, but it won't hurt to file away what your father is saying for future reference."

"Tomorrow Chuck leaves for the wheat ranch and will be gone all summer," Mr. Richards continued. "You two can choose a lonely time of missing each other or you can broaden your relationships by meeting new friends and enjoying a variety of personalities. You may find that this makes you appreciate each other even more. If not, you will be glad that you found out before taking any serious step into an unhappy future."

Mr. Richards pulled up into the parking lot before the falls. Chuck and Jonie walked quietly from the car and gazed upward at the magnificent display of white water. Little springs trickled down forested mountain slopes, across alpine meadows, and through cool ravines, forming at last the singing stream of rushing water finding its way to the wide Columbia River. Cascading over a great cliff at its destination's edge, the long wedding veil of sheer spray was crowned with a double rainbow. Standing near the sculptured rock bowl of sunlit, dancing waters, Jonie felt the mist on her face and photographed the beauty in her mind. Chuck reached for her hand, and together they hiked the trail to the top of the falls from where they could see the mighty Columbia flowing through the Cascade Range and distant evergreens and on to the sea.

For a few quiet moments they stood viewing the natural east-west travel route of tiny tugboats, occasional freighters, and, here and there, a billowing sail. A long sigh escaped from Jonie.

"I'll miss you terribly, you know."

"Not the way I'll miss you," Chuck responded.

"Come on, now! The farmer probably has a beautiful daughter." She was smiling, but the words were not teasing.

"Jonie, I've loved only one girl. I doubt that will ever change," Chuck answered seriously.

Jonie was silent.

"Maybe Dad has a point." He looked at her, willing her to disagree.

"He is right, you know," Jonie said softly.

"Yes, but we've invested a lot of precious years in this relationship. I remember the first time I walked into that grade-school room, the first time I ever laid eyes on you. I said to myself, That's the girl I'm going to marry someday!"

Jonie's sudden burst of merry laughter scattered a few quail lurking in the bushes. "Oh, Chuck, that skinny little girl?"

"She was beautiful to me," he answered.

"How many times since kindergarten have you told yourself you'd found *the one?*" she teased.

He looked into her amused eyes steadily for a moment, then said quietly, "Only once."

Jonie looked away. It was difficult to face the real issue. "You've never told me this before." She paused, looking down the river, hearing the wisdom of Mr. Richards' words ringing in her mind. "Your dad *is right,* you know."

Chuck's arm tightened about her waist. "I know," he answered, looking down into her eyes. "I know what you're going to tell me. You're going to agree with Dad that we should call it off for a while, and I don't want to face that."

"But you know our love hasn't stood still. It does

continue to grow, and controlling the feelings within us while we face a long wait is a real strain on both of us."

"Are you trying to tell me that's what is causing the tensions between us?"

"Well, we have been quarreling," she stated.

"Yes," he sighed. "I know what you mean. But we will be separated all summer."

"And just living for the day when we see each other again. What then? A replay of the same, a struggle with our emotions all over again? for the next three or four years? No, Chuck, I can't live with that and I won't live with a guilty conscience. I want you the same way you want me. At the right time, in the right place, and with a commitment before God."

There was silence. Chuck spoke finally, his words barely audible. "You want to break up?"

"Not really. Oh, Chuck, not really, but I feel certain it's probably for the best. For now, anyway."

"For how long?"

"We'll know when the right time comes."

"And, meanwhile, I run the risk of losing you." His voice sounded hurt and angry.

"I'm taking the same risk," Jonie answered.

"I doubt that."

"Much has been said about the test of time," she reminded him.

"Well, don't tell me about it. Just look at a few of our friends. Time and separations didn't help most of them to remain couples!" He fairly spat the words out.

"I guess if our feelings for each other don't last they aren't worth much."

"*Last?* While you grow fonder of someone else?" he said angrily.

"Oh, Chuck, be reasonable. Casual friendships with other people will only make us appreciate each other more in the end."

"Unless we find somebody else."

"Then it would be better if we never marry each other or lock ourselves into a relationship of premarital sex."

"Have I ever asked for that?"

"No, but I feel it out there taunting us like some demon too close for comfort. I love you, Chuck," Jonie cried out. "And boys aren't the only ones with problems. My feelings are just as deep and just as strong."

For a long time, neither spoke. Jonie's throat ached, and her ribs hurt with the strength of Chuck's tightened grasp. Finally she stood free of his touch, wishing love did not have to be so painful.

He turned and brushed past her, taking the trail back down into the gorge.

"Please," she petitioned, reaching out to touch his arm. "Does it have to be like this? Can't we be friends?"

He halted without turning. "Friends!"

She was walking toward him, and he turned suddenly and kissed her with a finality that bruised her heart. She followed him silently back down the trail, praying over and over again that she wasn't making a mistake.

Chuck would be leaving in the morning, and at the bakery that night Jonie's mind was far from her work. Methodically, she sorted, wrapped, iced, and performed her tasks with little interest. She appreciated being alone rather than having a full crew bustling noisily about. For the most part the great machines were still, and the quietness was soothing. Only the bread wrapper banging away in another room broke the silence.

A batch of thick, unwieldy icing brought Jonie out of her pensive reverie and she hurried back to the adjoining storage-and-sink room. She switched on the light and passed through the narrow aisle between large bags of flour stacked to the ceiling. The air was stifling hot. "Whew!" she muttered aloud. "Why don't they ever open the window back here?" She unlocked the back door that opened into the alley and left it ajar while she found a pail and scooped powdered milk base into it. Stepping up on the six-inch platform, she turned on the water at the long metal sink. With a wire whip, she noisily stirred and beat the frothy liquid to the consistency she wanted. Preoccupied, she did not hear the screen door open quietly and was not aware of the man who entered until he grabbed her from behind.

Jonie felt a moment of terror as the stranger's hands traveled up her body toward her throat. Following the initial shock, rage swept through her. She swung her left arm, still holding the full bucket, in an arc across the front of her body and up around the side of her head in a motion so fast the bucket never lost a drop until it caught the stranger full in the face. At the same instant, she flung her body backward against his. Momentarily blinded, the intruder lost his balance and fell off the platform as the milk hit the ceiling and cascaded in a shower over him and the flour-coated floor.

"Carl!" Jonie screamed, though she knew full well the man at the bread wrapper could not hear her. The stranger struggled to his feet, slipping and stumbling as he ran the short distance to the door then out into the alley. Quickly, Jonie slammed and locked the door behind him. She leaned against the wall, trembling. Looking up at the ceiling, she gazed at the wet spot and cried out, "God, where are You? My whole world's falling apart!"

A Singing Partner

IT WAS 12:30 A.M. when Jonie punched the time clock and checked out. She waved goodbye to the kindly old man who operated the bread wrapper and slipped through the front door.

The middle of the street seemed safer to Jonie than the shadowy sidewalk and she raced the few blocks to the well-lighted corner where she would catch the twelve-forty-five bus. Her heart was pounding in her throat. Luckily, there's no traffic on this side street tonight, she thought.

It was not until she sat down in the bus that she realized she was trembling all over. *Oh, Father, thank You, thank You for being with me. And go with Chuck in the morning. I love him so.*

Home at last, Jonie fell wearily into bed but her mind was still spinning with troubled thoughts: I can't tell my folks, for they will worry. But I can't go through this again. I'll have to figure out something different. With her eyes on the moonlit sky, she prayed, "Please work this one out, too, Father." Her eyes closed in relaxation, and she fell asleep.

All week Jonie was bothered by a little worm of concern. Her folks would be gone again this weekend, and she couldn't see her way out of the Saturday-night work situation. She was now well aware of the dangers involved in even the short walk to the bus so late at night. Thursday morning she finally gave up her concern and handed it over to the Lord. "I'm tired of thinking about all this, Father. If You've got a better plan I surely need to know about it."

At noon Mr. Milway spotted Jonie taking off her apron. "Say, young lady, how about stepping in here a minute?" He held open his office door and Jonie walked toward him, smiling as she shook her hair loose from its net. Mr. Milway was an old friend of her father's, and he had helped her get her summer job.

"How would you like to earn money with that smile of yours?" he asked as he pulled out a chair for her.

"I don't understand," she replied.

"Well, I'd like to send you on a country route that needs building up. The salesman delivers from door to door out there, and while he's making a delivery to one home, you can stop off at another, leave a loaf of bread and maybe a half dozen assorted cookies and perhaps make a new customer. You could help the salesman out by keeping up with the charges and cash received, adding a new page for each new customer and, in general, updating his book."

"Would I make as much as I am now?" Jonie asked uncertainly.

"Better. I'll even give you a small bonus on each new steady customer."

Suddenly, it dawned on Jonie that God was answering her prayer, and delight lighted up her face.

"You like the idea, I can see." Mr. Milway chuckled. "Then, we'd better break the new girl in on your job today and tomorrow. Monday morning you report to me at 7:00 A.M. sharp."

"Yes, sir!" Jonie answered happily.

Jonie was excited and a little nervous Monday morning. It will be fun talking to people, giving them something, and making friends, she thought.

"Now, Jonie," Mr. Milway said, shutting the door. "I have another reason for sending you out on this particular route, and this is between you and me. I want you to do a little sleuthing for me. If the salesman goes into a customer's house and stays longer than seems necessary I want you to make a small notation in the book. Just a little checkmark is fine. There is something that just doesn't add up here. Darren has shorter routes and fewer customers than some of the other drivers, and yet he seems to take much longer, especially on Tuesdays and Thursdays and once in a while on Mondays. I've asked why, but he's very noncommittal. Now, you're a clever girl and I'm sure you can manage this without his knowing what you're doing."

But Jonie wasn't so sure. When Mr. Milway took her out to the truck and made the introductions, Darren nodded politely, but looked startled when it was explained that she would be riding with him all day to solicit customers. When he shifted the noisy gears and started out he wasn't exactly friendly to the girl sitting beside him.

Oh, oh, thought Jonie. I can see I'm not too welcome. I'm not so sure I like being the bakery's FBI.

She sneaked a few hurried glances at Darren. She had seen very little of him before now, since he was always one of the first to load up and take to the road. Must not be more than two or three years older than I am, she thought. Wonder if he's guessed why I'm on this new assignment. Oh, dear, why doesn't he say something?

But Darren concentrated on starting, stopping, shifting, turning corners, and obviously ignoring her.

Finally, he reached over and turned on the radio. Instantly the cab was filled with the rich strains of classical music. Well, long hair! thought Jonie, with surprise. Wonder what else he likes. Maybe I should ask. Normally, she would have, but something about Darren's behavior inhibited her.

"Like music?" he shouted, without looking in her direction as they bumped over the ruts on a back road.

"Of course." Jonie was startled by this sudden brief communication.

"I mean real music," he shouted again.

"Why not?" she shouted back.

He nodded, then concentrated on his driving.

Presently, he caught her attention again. "How about Ezio Pinza, Lily Pons, Enrico Caruso, Patrice Munsel?"

Opera? Jonie raised the eyebrows, wishing she had paid more attention to her mother's great love.

He smiled. "Mind if I vocalize? I'm studying voice when I can afford the lessons."

"Go right ahead," Jonie said. Suddenly, with the orchestration blaring on the radio, Darren's voice soared in an operatic aria that sent chills down her spine and made her forget the ruts in the road.

With an abrupt turn to the right, the truck followed a long narrow drive to a tall Victorian home set back from the road. At the back door, the singing, the radio and the car all stopped with a twist of the key. Darren hopped out as four children and a heavyset woman came down the steps to the truck. They took in six loaves of bread, three pies, and two packages of rolls. Jonie made a notation of the charges in the book as Darren started the engine again.

"Good customers. They have quite a crew on the farm, and she doesn't have time to bake much. The next place has neighbors if you want to try them," he shouted as they took off again.

At the shabby farmhouse Jonie tried the front and back doors. A bathrobe-clad woman holding a cup of coffee finally answered. She smiled when she saw the cinnamon buns the girl offered as a get-acquainted gift and sent her hurrying back to the truck for two loaves of bread and a chocolate cream pie. As the woman paid for them, she asked to be included as a regular customer.

There were several other pleased housewives who welcomed Jonie before the morning was over, and Darren suddenly became alarmed when he realized he might be running short on bakery products before seeing his final customer.

"I guess tomorrow you will have to bring a bit more," Jonie said.

"Looks that way," Darren answered as he backed out of a driveway. Again they were bumping along. Jonie had been running all morning, squeezing in as many introductory calls as possible during each stop, trying not to hold Darren up and trying to do her job with the charge book. She was beginning to feel very hungry.

"Do you stop for lunch?" she shouted in between stanzas.

"Never," Darren replied loudly.

"Never?"

"Oh, I open some rolls or cookies sometimes."

"Fine way to treat a great artist."

Darren looked at her quickly and decided that she wasn't teasing.

"I've got a huge lunch. If you care to stop I'll share it with you. Of course, if you don't care to stop I could feed it to you in between arias or at least stuff your face when you come up for air."

Now, for sure, there was a bit of mischief in her voice.

The truck came to an abrupt halt. Jonie was pulling a brown bag from behind the seat, and looking up, she saw tall green grass, a rock wall, and behind it a small country church and cemetery.

She opened the truck door and sat holding the sack and staring at the picturesque scene before her. "I don't believe it," she said. "Why is it guys like to eat in graveyards?"

"Because the women don't talk," Darren answered slyly.

"Just for that I should make you sing for your dinner, but I prefer the crows."

"Now I know what you think of my voice," he said, leading the way to the low rock wall, where they found a shady place to sit and share the sandwiches and fruit.

"I truly think your voice is wonderful. I keep wondering what you plan to do with it."

"Haven't decided yet. What are your plans for the future?"

"College next year. Maybe I'll teach someday." Jonie bit into a shiny red apple and gazed across the road at the rolling green meadows and a field of golden grain ripening beyond. She wondered about Chuck and whether her future would include him.

When they arrived back at the bakery Jonie helped Darren carry in the few items that were left. They arranged them on the shelf and marked them day-old goods. When they were finished, he drove away hurriedly without saying goodbye. She turned to see Mr. Milway watching her, his eyebrows raised in question. She shrugged her shoulders in reply, realizing she had not accomplished what she was sent out to do.

New Suitcase

JONIE GAVE her battered suitcase a shove with her foot. Disgustedly, she muttered, "You miserable thing. I hate to buy a new one. It isn't that I couldn't part with you, it's just that I've got to save all I can for college."

She closed the case and walked to the full-length mirror. While zippering the soft-blue dress she turned sideways to check her nylons and the back of her shiny dark hair. She would have to hurry to catch that next bus to Linda's. She started for the front door just as the doorbell rang. Setting the suitcase down, Jonie ran, hoping not to be detained. She opened the door to a handsome young man in Navy uniform.

He tipped his cap and smiled. "You must be Miss Owens."

"That's right," she hesitated. "Should I know you?"

"We've never met, but our fathers are friends from way back. Mine wanted me to stop by and say Hello to yours on my way through. I'm Randy Wade."

"I'm Jonie, and I've heard my father speak of a Will Wade."

"That's the one." Randy flashed a captivating smile.

"Well, I'd be happy to invite you in, but my parents aren't here and I was about to catch a bus myself." She glanced nervously at her watch.

Randy sized up the situation and decided that the least he could do was to help this pretty girl. Having made the decision, he spoke quickly, "Please let me give you a lift."

Jonie hesitated, but only momentarily, as she heard the bus leave the corner where she should have been waiting.

"All right, but it's about six miles from here."

"No problem."

"Thank you so much."

Jonie hurried to get her bag, handed it to him, and locked the door. Being accompanied down the sidewalk and assisted into a car by someone in uniform was a new experience. Randy was very tall and very gallant. She was glad she had on her highest heels and secretly hoped the neighbors were watching.

He started the engine, and Jonie's feeling of shyness disappeared with the first two miles. Randy was very entertaining, and she was soon laughing at his clever wit. They exchanged ancient histories and acquainted each other with the present tenses of their lives.

"Are you in any big hurry to get to your friend's?" he asked.

"Not really. They do expect me before bedtime, though. Why?"

"I wondered whether you'd care to have dinner with me somewhere before I take you there?"

"I'd enjoy that," Jonie smiled. Randy selected a restaurant, and they continued their conversation over candlelight, with Randy describing some of the remote and exotic places he had visited. "Would you care for anything to drink?" he questioned as the waiter approached.

"No, thank you," Jonie said politely, but not without some concern. Just how much drinking would Randy do and how would it affect his driving? she wondered silently, sending a plea Heavenward.

He studied her face a moment then replied to the waiter's inquiry, "Two 7-Ups, please."

Jonie relaxed, and enjoyed the dinner and the very entertaining young man.

They arrived at Linda's about dusk, and Jonie was pleasantly aware of being observed from behind the curtains. As Randy opened the car door she stepped out gracefully and enjoyed this short tableau that was bound to be raising a few eyebrows indoors. Linda's younger sister would be full of questions.

"It's been a lovely evening, and you are a lovely girl," said Randy, lifting her suitcase from the trunk.

"Thank you. I've enjoyed every moment myself." Jonie's eyes glowed, but as he set the suitcase on the curb her bubble burst. The relic popped open, and numerous personal articles tumbled out on the sidewalk. After a moment of stunned immobility, the two of them scooped up nylons, night clothes, and underwear. Jonie's face was burning, and she could almost hear the laughter behind the curtains.

Randy hastily latched the case and walked Jonie to the door, assuring her it could happen to anyone.

But to Jonie, it happened twice! The repeat performance occurred at the door when everything, including her toothbrush, fell out.

Linda's 14-year-old sister opened the door to find two young people laughing uproariously, though one of them had a very red face.

Needless to say, Jonie's next purchase was a new suitcase.

Flying High

JONIE ENJOYED her new job, but was puzzled over Darren's attitude. He was not unpleasant, but she did detect something akin to resentment. Did he consider her an intruder? As for the assignment by Mr. Milway, she had been so busy route-building that she had not noticed anything unusual on Darren's part—timewise. By the second Tuesday she knew she must concentrate on any delays along the way.

At two o'clock that afternoon Darren stopped the truck at the side of the road, filled a basket with goods, and without any explanation, walked up the drive to a house.

"That's funny. We've never been here before." Jonie checked the book. Customer all right, but they don't buy much. Darren rang the bell and was admitted as Jonie watched from the road. Thirty minutes went by. She made a tiny check by the name. Ten minutes later, Darren came back and tried to make up the lost time by driving faster than usual.

In the few days Jonie had been soliciting new customers, Darren's workload had almost doubled. On Wednesday it looked as if he might not finish the route in time for his voice lesson. This inspired him to begin practicing again, and once more his soaring arias floated over the countryside. No explanation was made for the long stop, but similar incidents happened twice on Thursday. Jonie made more notations, suddenly feeling like a tattletale.

"If Mr. Milway wants an explanation of Darren's time, I sure couldn't give it," she mused. When she thought the situation over, there was one thing that kept coming to mind. Each time Darren got out of the truck on one of his "long visits" he reached under the seat for something. Quickly, Jonie checked there herself, but produced nothing.

She got out of the truck and went up the drive. A little uncertainly, she knocked at the back door. Through the glass pane she could see the woman of the house and her three children looking at something Darren was pointing to in a book. He glanced up, startled, as the woman called out a greeting.

Darren's face relaxed as Jonie joined the widow and her children about the table.

When they were back in the car he slipped his Bible under the seat, and Jonie said, "Why didn't you tell me what you do when you're gone so long? That was tremendous! You have such a convincing, persuasive power with the Word of God."

"That was the Holy Spirit at work, Jonie."

"I know, but you were certainly His instrument." Suddenly, a new, vibrant Darren emerged as he told of his studies with each of his interested contacts.

"Darren, how can I help?"

"You want to?" He flashed her a smile.

"Of course."

"I appreciate all the extra customers and the extra commissions, but it's really rough trying to get everything squeezed into each day. Could you drive to a few houses while I am having a study?"

Jonie's face fell. "I don't have a license."

"Oh. Well, on these back roads you'd be safe enough. All the farm kids are driving these roads before they should."

"But, Darren, I don't know how to drive," she wailed.

"Then I guess I'd better teach you. Scoot over," he said, stopping the truck and getting out to take her place on the other side of the cab. "Now let me show you how to shift this beast."

Jonie was not at all excited about this turn of events, but since it was for a good cause, she would give it her best. They took off jerkily with Jonie trying to manage the gears and stay on the road. The steering column seemed stiff and awkward in her clenched grasp.

"There's our next house, Jonie. Turn to the right."

Jonie began to turn, then suddenly swerved to the left. Darren grabbed the wheel, pulling to the right.

"Don't hit the cat!" Jonie shouted, and yanked it again to the left. They missed the road, flew across a ditch and out into a field before she stomped on the brake.

With the sudden stop, three pies flew forward from the shelf above, and when Jonie turned to look at Darren he was bearded in white topping and crowned with butterscotch.

"Oh, no! Oh, no!" she said, horror stricken, then began to laugh and cry all at once as Darren sputtered, "I always did like butterscotch!"

He got out of the truck and headed across the field for the river. When he came back Jonie had the interior cleaned up with the help of a few friendly bees.

"How do we get out of here?" she asked as they took stock of the situation.

"How we got here is what I can't figure out." Darren shook his head. "We must have flown over that ditch."

"We did," she replied. "But we can't fly back."

"No, we'll have to make two narrow bridges of fill-in from that pile of rocks, enough to get the wheels across." They drove up to the edge of the narrowest width of the ditch and began carrying stones. They resented the extra time loss, but were grateful that the damage was only three pies.

After some pretty heavy labor they were back on the road again, Darren at the wheel.

"Darren," Jonie said meekly, "I'd really rather not drive illegally."

"I think you're right," he answered.

As the weeks progressed, Jonie's added customers swelled the workload, and sales climbed. She assisted by delivering to nearby houses whenever possible so Darren would have time for the studies.

In her report to Mr. Milway, she said the time problem had merely been a matter of reorganization and everything seemed in order. He smiled and commended her for helping to make that one of the better routes. She was glad he had not heard of the near disaster.

In due time Darren accepted Jonie as a working partner and became a bit more communicative. She, in turn, found herself more and more appreciative of his world of music. One bright morning he drove the route at such a pace that she wondered over the extreme haste and had difficulty keeping up with the speed with which he made deliveries. When she pulled out her lunch at noon he said, "I hope you don't mind eating on the run, but I'd like to finish up before stopping today."

"Fine with me," she said, handing him a sandwich.

It was shortly after three o'clock when they saw the last customer, but instead of turning toward town,

Darren drove in another direction. Jonie assumed it must be a new Bible study until he pulled up in front of the county fair. "I thought we deserved some fun for a change," he said, looking for a parking place.

"You are so right," Jonie agreed. "Darren, look, turn over by that gate and stop for a moment, please. I have an idea." She jumped out and ran over to a food concession. Darren saw her talking to a rotund man in a white chef's cap. Soon she hurried back smiling, with the man close behind her.

"Darren, open the back of the truck. This gentleman wants to see what all we have left. I told him he can have it all at a discount so we don't have to take it back to the bakery."

Darren shook his head, laughing at her. "Leave it to you, Jonie."

"Now, there are two, or maybe three, cakes up there," she said, pointing to the top shelf. The chef nodded as he took the remaining cakes, mentally adding up the profit per slice. He also bought the rest of the bread, pies, and several dozen donuts.

"Now, if you like, we could stop by each day throughout the fair and see how you're doing."

"That will be just fine. If business keeps up like it has today, you will be more than welcome." The round face beamed.

They helped carry the goods to his outdoor kitchen and hurried happily on to the Ferris wheel. It was two tired and relaxed young people who left the fair that evening. A plush teddy bear sporting a large polka-dotted bow tie was being cuddled by Jonie. Darren had won it with a few dimes and some skilled marksmanship.

David

THE GLADSTONE CAMPGROUND was a small city of cabins, tents, and campers. It also included a large cafeteria, bookstore, grocery store, business offices, welfare building, and choir hall, besides the numerous meeting pavilions for the more than twenty thousand members who would be attending in the parklike setting.

Jonie had attended Oregon camp meeting for the first time when she was 7 and had not missed a year since that time. On these very grounds she had graduated from the little eight-grade church school. This was where she had met Chuck. How she wished he were with her now.

She hurried from the shower house back to the tent to dress for the evening meeting. The large family tents were mounted on wooden frames set on a wood floor with board walls extending a third of the way up. The inside was divided into rooms with curtain partitions. Jonie's family had left for the service. In her own small portion of the tent, she dressed quickly, listening for the meeting bell and hoping Linda would arrive before it was time to go. She was brushing her hair vigorously when there was a rap on the framing at the doorway of the tent.

"Come," she called, then added happily, "I'm so glad you made it."

"Are you?" a masculine voice answered softly.

Jonie's heart skipped a beat. It was a voice she had not heard for a year. Trembling slightly, she stepped out from behind the curtain and found David. She smiled shyly and reached out her hand.

"Jonie! It's good to see you!" David said, squeezing the proffered palm. "I still remember that scent."

"Scent?" she said, puzzled.

He laughed softly. "Yes. You always had a fragrance about you like some white flower just after a rain."

"Why, thank you, but I'm afraid it's nothing more exotic than soap."

"Perhaps, but it's a part of you I hadn't forgotten."

"Where have you been?" Jonie asked. "We've all missed you."

"And I've missed you very much. I've been working on a ranch in Idaho and when I heard about camp meeting here in Oregon I couldn't resist coming over and looking up my good friends the Owenses and a few others."

At that moment Linda appeared at the door flap, and Jonie hastily introduced her to David.

"Linda, remember the stories I've told you about riding horses and selling books and eating supper in the graveyard in Arizona? Well, this is David, the one I shared all those unforgettable experiences with. Now, you two sit down and get acquainted while I finish my hair."

Jonie ducked behind the curtain and picked up the hairbrush, suddenly realizing that she was shaking badly. "Get hold of yourself," she whispered to the mirror wired to a nail in the framing. "How do I handle this? He does care, and I don't want to hurt such a dear friend. Maybe he and Linda will find each other interesting and fun. That's it!" She gave her hair a final pat, and on a sudden impulse crawled over the boarded side wall and slipped quietly away, leaving the two guests talking in the front of the tent.

Presently the bell for the evening meeting rang, and Linda called out in puzzlement, "Jonie, are you ready?" When there was no answer, she stepped behind the curtain and exclaimed, "Why, she's not here!"

David looked disturbed. "Well, let's wait a few minutes. Maybe she'll be back," he answered.

"Yes, she probably went over to the restroom." But Linda had her doubts, knowing that Jonie would have had to crawl over the wall.

They waited until the song service was under way and then left for the meeting.

Meanwhile, Jonie hurried toward the woods and the pond that was overgrown with lily pads. Once there, she sank down on the grass and listened to the *galump-croak* music of the evening while her mind spun off on a tangent. Her heart was beating hard from the hike and the thoughts of the capricious thing she had just done.

"Father, I know that was stupid," she whispered. "I should never have run away, but Linda is the loveliest girl I know, and David is so very good. Maybe You could work things out for them." She sat there for a few more moments. "OK, Lord, I know I belong in the meeting." She stood up, smoothed down the pink-and-white cotton skirt and tucked in the dainty white Swiss blouse. Tossing back her long dark hair, she retraced her steps and arrived at the meeting just as the speaker took his place on the platform.

Jonie glanced over the crowd of young people and spotted David and Linda on the end of a bench, lustily singing the opening song from a shared book. She slipped in beside them. David smiled a greeting, and

Linda raised her eyebrows in question. Jonie greeted them casually, then glanced toward the platform as though nothing was amiss, feeling sure God would take care of her dilemma.

Friday night and Sabbath were full of spiritual blessings and the pleasures of meeting many old friends. Jonie's parents and her younger brother, Jimmy, were delighted to have David join them. After dinner Jonie heard her father invite David to go with a hiking group that was planning to scale Mount Hood in the early morning. She hurried out of the tent, exclaiming, "Who's climbing Mount Hood? I've always wanted to climb that mountain."

The two men laughed. "And why do you want to climb Mount Hood?" her father asked, winking at David.

"I'm serious," she said. "Mother did it when she was in her teens, so I don't see why I can't. You know I like to climb. And, besides, camp meeting will be over, and it will be fun to have an outing before going home."

"OK. We are driving up there tonight. If your mother doesn't mind I guess we'll put up with you."

Jonie grinned in delight as she turned to receive a nod of approval from her mother. "It's all right with me as long as your brother helps move our things out of here in the morning," said Donna Owens. She was secretly pleased that Jonie was interested in the climb.

"Fine with me," Jimmy said, sneaking five olives from the table.

Late that night the group hiked the lower summits under the stars, found a grassy meadow, and bedded down for a few hours' rest before attacking the lofty precipice above.

The first rays of light ushered in high adventure for

the would-be mountaineers, who soon left timberline trees silhouetted behind them in the rosy dawn. Mount Hood is a mountain of many moods. It stands stalwart against the Pacific storms and holds back needed rains from the parched, sagebrush-covered valleys of eastern Oregon.

On this particular morning, the mountain wore a halo of white clouds that promised to lift as the day progressed. The highest of all Oregon mountains, Hood's 11,245 feet were challenging to the amateur mountain climbers. The lower trails offered an intimate association with nature through the beauty of plant and animal life as they continued on to the highest slopes of ever-changing grandeur. Later, when they stopped to rest, Jonie felt there was nothing that could compare with a sparkling drink from a glacier-fed, clear-water stream.

Sulfur steam rising from the deep crevasse was not the most pleasant odor, and Jonie felt a bit nauseated for a short time. The climb through the clouds was somewhat damp, but finally the ascent took them into the sunlight, where gleaming ridges and volcanic cones reached out of the clouds and high into the blue heavens.

The last peak to be scaled was almost straight up. Jonie had come to the end of her strength. She watched the others climbing hand over hand by rope up the perpendicular face of Hood and felt like crying. "I'll never, never make it," she said dejectedly to herself. "I never will. I'm just too tired. But I *must*. I've come this far and I've got to."

Her father was next in line. "Come on, honey. Follow me," he called.

Reluctantly, Jonie took her place, grabbed the rope, dug her feet into the rock and began a wriggling, caterpillarlike ascent."

"Oh, Father, please help me. Help me, please. I've got to make it." Why it was so important she could not tell. Bone weary, she struggled on, muscles straining and cramping from the unaccustomed abuse, her energy derived from raw determination. For years to come it was the mettle tested in those moments by which she measured herself.

Her father, over the edge of the top, turned to give her a hand. David stood waiting as she struggled up the last few feet. Congratulations and backslapping followed, but Jonie could think of nothing but the view. The clouds had scattered, and one could follow the Cascade Range to the sea or the mighty Columbia River, like a blue ribbon, across the green-velvet valley.

Close at hand was a pile of boards that had once been a cabin, long ago destroyed by the winds of many storms. Chained to the debris was a metal box containing the logbook. In it, each mountain climber wrote the date and his name, feeling an exhilerating sense of accomplishment on seeing it there in black and white.

Exhausted, Jonie was glad to sit down by David and share a sandwich and some hot chocolate. She was too tired to talk much, but gazed quietly into the far distance at the calico patchwork of deep-brown earth, golden grain, and green alfalfa. She imagined she could see the farm where Chuck was working and hear the din of the great trucks into whose gaping beds he would be shoveling wheat.

Her thoughts were interrupted when David spoke. "I'm planning to go to college, Jonie."

A pleased smile brightened her face. "One very wise decision, I'd say. I hope you don't put it off for long. I always felt that you had so much talent to give the world."

"College is expensive, you know," he said.

"But so important! I heard it said once that if you knew Jesus was coming in three years, you should spend two of them getting a good education and you would accomplish that much more during the third."

He nodded thoughtfully. "Of course, it makes sense to be well prepared."

"That's right, and I know once you are prepared your opportunities will be limitless. I really believe in you, David."

"Well, maybe with God's help your faith will see its reward."

"I know it will. I wish I could hear your first sermon, should you go into the ministry."

He smiled, looking away. "I'd like that," he said softly into the wind.

"David," she said, and then paused, looking earnestly at the young man beside her. The wind played gently in her hair, and David saw not the girl of the past, but the woman she was becoming, and he knew it was not to Jonie he must prove his worth, but to himself and, ultimately, to his heavenly Father. It was only through His Son that the long struggle to reach that goal of being a minister would be accomplished. Jonie continued, "If it should be a very long time before we see each other again, you will always be in my thoughts and prayers. You are one of the finest young men I have met—or ever will meet." His eyes met hers, and he had no doubt as to her sincerity.

"Thank you, Jonie. Your faith has always given me courage." He reached over and squeezed her hand, then rubbed the chilly fingers between his broad palms till they were warm again.

Going down the cliff was a breeze compared to the effort expended on the rope going up. But once at the bottom, hiking through the snow was so wearisome that

Jonie's legs ached and trembled. I should have gotten in
condition for this, she thought. Ol' muscleman there
will never know what this is like for me. David is so
disgustingly fit, who could ever keep up with him? A bit
of envy was mixed with her grumbling.

On a steep decline, Jonie found a wide, smooth, short
board. She sat down and it slid nicely. Soon she was
skimming over the snow with more fun than effort.
"Way to go!" someone shouted as she whizzed by the
group that was lagging behind. She soon caught up with
David and sailed by, waving smugly as she passed.

Jonie didn't realize that somewhere along the way
she had lost the board and was sliding along neatly on
the seat of her pants. The warm sunshine aided in
making a slick path, and the dampness soaked through
one pair of red wool slacks and two pairs of long
underwear. Below, on the alpine meadows of wild-
flowers, she stood up and looked back to discover a faded
red trail above her and her slacks almost completely
worn through to the numbness she could almost feel
beneath.

Donna Owens and Jimmy had hiked part way up to
meet the group, and together they descended the rest of
the way to the waiting car.

Jimmy wanted his sister to go to the youth skating
party that night, but her only response was a groan.
Eager to be helpful, he reached into the glove compart-
ment and produced a bottle of liniment.

"Look, Sis! Just the elixir-fixer cureall for your aches
and groans. I brought it especially for you. Now, if you
will shove up the long johns, I'll rub those aching
muscles and you'll be good as new."

With that, he pulled out the cork and the air
instantly reeked with a pungent, unfamiliar odor.

"Jimmy, no, you don't! *No, you don't!*" Jonie shouted

in alarm. "No one will get near me for a month if I use that stuff!" She was pulling her clothes back down to her boot tops.

"Come on, Sis. This bottle has great promises in it. And you love to skate."

"But I'll never get rid of the odor," she complained.

"Sure, you will. Just use some of mom's bubble bath."

"Well," Jonie hesitated uncertainly, but Jimmy reached down for her boot, lifted it to his thigh and generously applied the odoriferous liquid to her bared calf muscles. The penetrating heat gave instant comfort.

The odor inspired many remarks on the way home, but Jonie slept through most of them, and after a pleasant and relaxing bubble bath she agreed to the skating party, to her father's amazement and Jimmy's pleasure.

David was also pleased. He was leaving in the morning, so it would be their last evening together. He smiled rather oddly as he carried her skates out the door to the car.

"What's the matter?" Jonie questioned him uncertainly.

"He's enjoying your skunk cabbage cologne," Jimmy said.

"Oh, no! I'm not going," Jonie balked.

"Come on, Sis. We can stick our heads out the window."

"David, do I really smell like skunk cabbage?"

"Not at all," he answered seriously. "More like dead possum."

"That does it!" and Jonie flew back into the house.

David and Jimmy ran after her, intent on convincing her they were only teasing, and soon they were on their way.

It was an evening of activity and music, with the added fun of meeting many young people from the associated youth group representing more than a dozen churches. Jimmy met some old friends and rode home with them when it was over.

David took Jonie home by way of the river road. A moonlit path shimmered on the water, and they rode in weary silence, enjoying the tranquillity of the beautiful night. David rolled the window down and took a deep breath. "Ummmm, smell that Oregon country. Pine needles and white blossoms," he said, glancing sideways at Jonie.

"Any dead possum," she muttered.

He chuckled, reaching out his hand for hers. "Truce?"

"Uh huh." She smiled. "I'm glad you came to Oregon camp meeting, David, and I'll always remember today and Mount Hood. Such an accomplishment!" she exclaimed.

"May I ask you something?" he said.

"Of course."

"When you left Arizona last year and went back to Columbia Academy, was it because of Chuck?"

She hesitated, then answered sincerely, "He was part of the reason, as were all my friends. It was my class, my school, and soon I shall feel that way about Walla Walla College as I become a part of it and it becomes a part of me."

"Jonie?" He spoke her name quietly and like a question.

"Yes," she answered, her heart beginning to quicken.

"You are in love with Chuck, aren't you?"

For a moment she didn't speak and then, in all honesty, answered his question. "Yes. I guess I have been for a long time."

"I thought so." There was silence for a moment and presently David's hand withdrew from hers and returned to the steering wheel.

Jonie's eyes looked to the stars and her heart to Heaven. She turned toward David and spoke gently, "How good God is to give us so much love. A cup brimming over with beautiful friendships. This one I have with you I shall always treasure, David."

"And so will I," he said, smiling at her.

That night they parted, not to meet again for many years. Jonie had hoped that a relationship would develop between David and Linda, and had turned the matter over to God. But it was not to be. There was another lovely girl meant for David. As for Jonie, she would treasure happy memories of their brief visit and would always be grateful that they parted as good friends.

New Customer

DARREN GRINNED as Jonie climbed gingerly into the bakery truck. "Those few days you took off for camp meeting really aged you."

"Oh, you mean I move a little stiffly. But it wasn't camp meeting. It was climbing Mount Hood. I found some new muscles on that trip."

They rode along companionably, sharing the activities of the past few days. When they reached the route territory, Jonie pointed to a small house overgrown with weeds. "Look, Darren, there is a car in front of that empty house. Maybe someone moved in. Could be a new customer." She grabbed a loaf of bread from the shelf behind her.

Darren pulled over and Jonie jumped out. "I'll go on to the first regular stop and then come back," he called as the truck moved away. Jonie ran up the path and knocked on the door. A girl about her age answered and looked startled as Jonie dropped the loaf of bread into her hands.

"Good morning. I'm Jonie Owens. That's just a moving-in gift to let you know about our convenient bakery service that delivers right to your door. You just moved in?"

"Yesterday."

"Good. Then I'll be seeing you twice a week if you're interested in our service. We have pastries and quite a variety of bakery goods."

The girl smiled. "I'm sure mother will be pleased, and thank you for the bread. Say, didn't I see you at camp meeting?"

It was Jonie's turn to be surprised. "If you mean Gladstone, I was there."

"I was sure of it! You came into the meeting Friday evening and sat with some friends. I was back a row with my mother." She hesitated, then added shyly, "I remember thinking, I wish I could get to know that girl. That's why I was so surprised when I saw you at the door."

"This is really nice," Jonie responded. "I'd love getting acquainted."

Back at the truck, she was bubbling over with news about the new customers, Lorrene Winning and her mother. "Darren, you've got to meet her. She's darling—kind of shy and lonely. They came here from the Midwest and found this house. Her father died, and now her mother is starting to work in Portland. Lorrene just graduated from high school and is looking for a job. She said she saw me at camp meeting."

"You mean they are church members?"

"No, I got the idea that they were just invited. Apparently they really enjoyed it, though. Maybe I could get her to go to college with me."

Darren laughed. "But, Jonie, you just met her. Do you always plan people's lives for them?"

"Only when I think they might be happier."

From then on, Jonie looked forward to Mondays and Thursdays, when she could spend a few moments with Lorrene. One Thursday Jonie invited the girl and her mother to church and dinner the following Sabbath.

Donna Owens found Dorothy Winning delightful company, and all the questions stored in Dorothy's heart were poured out to her newfound friends. She was seeking a closer walk with her Master and wished to be baptized by immersion as Jesus was.

Lorrene appreciated her mother's convictions, but was uncertain as to her own stand. Later in the afternoon the two girls shared confidences in Jonie's room. Lorrene listened to Jonie's enthusiasm about college in the fall and wistfully mentioned her own dreams for a college education, now set aside.

"I just have to get a job. I could have had one, but mother decided we should be keeping all ten of the commandments instead of only nine. I guess that's why she doesn't want me to work on Saturdays."

"You mean because the Bible says, 'Remember the sabbath day, to keep it holy'?"

Lorrene nodded. "Yes, and it's not that I don't want to do what God says, but that command was given way back in Old Testament times. This is today!"

Thoughtfully, Jonie answered her. "He also said not to kill or steal. Do you think He changed His mind about that also?"

Lorrene shook her head. "Of course not."

Jonie smiled, "I hardly think our God would change His mind about just one thing. In fact, I'm convinced that He is consistent in all things. Reach over on that nightstand and get my Bible."

Lorrene picked up the small white Book.

"Now, find the very last chapter and read verse fourteen."

Lorrene read aloud from Revelation. "'Blessed are they that do his commandments, that they may have right to the tree of life, and may enter in through the gates into the city.'" She slowly closed the Book, staring at Jonie in wonderment. "He really didn't change His mind, did He?"

"No, Lorrene. There's nothing wishy-washy about God. His own Son said that He came not to destroy the law, but to establish it. And another time, He said that not even any punctuation marks would be taken from the law. I believe in keeping the law, and I feel that sharing the Sabbath day with Him should be done in love. It's a precious sign between us, like a pact. The psalmist says, 'I delight to do thy will, O my God.'"

"Oh, Jonie, it's all becoming so plain! If He would just help me to find a job where I wouldn't have to work on His day."

Jonie lay staring at the ceiling, her dark hair spread over the pink ruffled pillow sham. Suddenly, she sat up. "I know what you can do!" she said excitedly. "Go to college and apply."

"For school?" Lorrene looked baffled.

"No. I mean, yes! Go and apply for work and classes. We'll pray about it. You wouldn't have Sabbath worries there."

Lorrene looked doubtful. "But do you think they would accept me?"

"Sure, why not? Anything is possible, and it's worth a try." Jonie rummaged briefly in a dresser drawer and then handed her school bulletin to the bewildered girl. "Now, don't telephone them and give them a chance to say No. Just pack up your things, get your mother to drive you there, and let them know you mean business. Tell them it's the only way you can go to school and that you are staying. Period."

Lorrene began to shake with sudden laughter. "Oh, Jonie," she gasped, "my mother would never do that!"

"Why, she will, too! We'll both be praying. I'm sure God wants you to have a Christian education and meet

Christian friends. He'll work it out."

"I do have a little money saved, but I was——"
Lorrene hesitated.

Jonie cut in. "Don't think about the buts or doubts.
Satan can give you a million of them. Come on, let's go
convince your mother."

With the encouragement of the Owenses, Dorothy
agreed to take her daughter to the college on the
following day if she could arrange for Monday off.

That night Jonie woke up several times and prayed
earnestly for her friend. Monday, as she and Darren
made their rounds, the blinds were pulled at the
Winnings' house and there was a note on the door. It
read, "No bread today. I guess you know why. Thanks
much. I love you. L. P.S. Keep your fingers crossed."

Jonie flew down the gravel path, waving the note at
Darren, who grinned with pleasure. "I guess we won't be
seeing her the rest of this summer," he stated. And then
he added in mock seriousness, "You sure know how to
get rid of customers."

Suddenly Jonie threw her arms around Darren's
waist and laughed joyously. He blushed a bit, and
looked confused at her unexpected behavior. "Jonie,
your spontaneous combustion overwhelms me."

She let go quickly, still laughing. "Darren, thank
you for believing as I do. I just know she won't be back
tomorrow. They will accept her! God will see to that."
And God did!

During the two and one-half months that remained
before freshman orientation in late September, Jonie
contacted enough new customers to build a third route.
The hours were long, and what spare time she had was
often spent at the sewing machine preparing her fall
and winter wardrobe. She didn't see Mrs. Winning,
because of her working hours, and often wondered how

Lorrene was doing. One day she discovered that the small house was again vacant.

Jonie's conscience pricked her. Except for one short letter from Lorrene telling of her acceptance, there had been no other communication. Even though Lorrene's note had sounded a bit lonely, Jonie was sure the girl would soon make friends and enjoy herself. She had neglected to answer the letter. Now she was concerned. As she stood in front of the vacant house, she had a feeling that all was not as it should be.

That night she wrote a long letter to Lorrene, in care of the college. Several days later, the letter was returned with no forwarding address. Jonie became alarmed. "Perhaps her mother has moved up near the school," Mrs. Owens suggested. "That's something I'd like to do if we were not returning to Arizona."

"I just don't know," Jonie replied. "I wish I had answered her letter."

Shortly before school began, she again heard from Lorrene. The letter filled her with dismay.

Dear Jonie,

I did not stay at the college very long. I found a better job, which included my room and board, so I moved away. It was nice there, but I was homesick and everyone was busy. No one seemed very friendly. I spent so much time in my room alone.

Then I met these wonderful friends who took me to some meetings. Everyone was so caring and our leader is such a wonderful man. I became involved and am now a follower.

Thank you for trying to help. I have found the way.

Love, Lorrene.

Tears filled Jonie's eyes. "What way? What way? Oh, Mother, I didn't write. I even forgot to pray, once she was settled."

"What's her address, Jonie?" Donna Owens said, reaching for the letter.

"There is none, only a Seattle postmark," Jonie cried.

Donna shook her head. "That poor girl has gotten herself mixed up with a cult. That must be where her mother went."

"She was so shy and lonely. If only someone at the college had befriended her. It would have been better if I hadn't talked her into going. She could have gone this fall when the rest of us did. Why did I rush her so?"

"Jonie, you were only helping her to get a job. You couldn't know this would happen, so quit blaming yourself."

"Well, I've sure learned one thing. I will be friendly to every poor lonely kid I ever see. And I just pray that I can somehow make up for this mistake."

The Walla Walla College Hello Walk was the place to begin, and Jonie's ever-ready smile won many friends among lonely students who came from all parts of the world. But always that missing, winsome face haunted her memories, for she never again saw Lorrene.

Freshmen Again

"GAIL, I'M so glad you came early," Jonie said, hugging her roommate warmly. "Everything looks so nice, and weren't we lucky to get a corner room where we can see out both directions on the campus?"

"Just like when we were freshmen the first time, only this time we can see the men's residence hall," Gail grinned.

"And the tennis courts just below the window this way," Jonie said, pulling back the crisp white-lace curtain and leaning forward to watch several students playing doubles.

Gail shook back her luxurious brown hair and went to work helping Jonie get settled. Her blue eyes sparkled with anticipated pleasure. Being together again meant much to both girls after sharing their academy years and a few summer letters.

On a sudden impulse Jonie whirled around and hugged her roommate again. She appreciated this mite of a girl who had a way of helping to keep her organized. Soon they were hunting up old friends on the campus and heading for the dinner line and a watermelon feed on the lawn outside the cafeteria. This brought the fellows and girls together for lively interaction. In the midst of the confusion Jonie came face to face with

Chuck. For a moment they stared at each other.

"Hi, how was your summer?" Jonie asked brightly. He was with several boys she didn't know, and she felt a little awkward.

"Great. How about yours?"

"Busy, but fun."

"That's good. Well, see you around!" With that, he walked away with his two companions.

"Who was *she*?" one of them exclaimed.

"Oh, the girl I used to go with. Let's sit down over there and eat our melon."

Rudy was watching Jonie walk back to her group. "Ummm, not bad," he said with appreciation. "Why'd you drop that one?"

"It wasn't my idea," Chuck muttered.

"Oh," Rudy paused, looking at Chuck, "you still like her, huh?"

"Maybe. Now, could we change the subject?"

Jonie, feeling a little short of breath, was grateful for the security of Gail, Linda, Beth, and Donna, all former classmates from Columbia Academy.

"Notice how the kids sort of group together with their own friends from various schools?" Donna said as Jonie seated herself.

"Yes, but that probably won't last long as we get better acquainted," Linda stated.

"You're right," Jonie answered. "We have two darling girls from Laurelwood next door to us, and I'm eager to get to know them."

"There's a girl eating all alone. I wonder who she is," Donna nodded toward a petite blonde sitting under a nearby tree.

Jonie put down her paper plate. "Come on, Donna, let's go see. I'd hate to go to bed thinking that someone was lonesome in this mob."

The two girls strolled over and introduced themselves. Carrie accepted the invitation to join their group, and they soon learned that her roommate had not arrived yet.

"I'll be glad when she gets here, but I'm sort of scared too."

"Really! Why?" Gail asked.

"Maybe she won't like me."

"She'll like you," Jonie said, reassuringly. "This must be your first time living away from home."

Carrie nodded. "Does it show that much?"

The girls laughed. "I think it always does," Gail answered. "And a roommate is pretty important. Four years ago Jonie got me, and she's been stuck ever since."

"Well, you don't hear me complaining," Jonie smiled at her.

Carrie studied them. "I never went to a boarding school. In fact, this is my first time in a Christian school of any kind. I envy the rest of you."

"I guess we sometimes don't realize how fortunate we are," Beth remarked. "I know I've done my share of griping."

"Haven't we all?" Donna added.

The following day was one of long registration lines, meeting with counselors, deciding on courses of study and getting them approved, and endless testing periods.

"Oh, Jonie, I heard that freshman English testing is the worst of all," said Gail, catching up with Jonie on the walk.

"Well, it couldn't be worse than the one we just got out of."

"Of course you'd think that, since you plan to take an English major. You love composition and anything journalistic, but I hate writing and if you flunk, you get stuck in Miss Hammond's bonehead English."

Maybe that one's easier if it's for boneheads," Jonie laughed.

"Easier! I heard she's a bear about making you really learn the basics and, not only that, the other courses run three days a week and bonehead English runs five days! Imagine English every day. What a waste! I'd better score on this one. I'd hate to get stuck with her class every day."

"Five days of English for the same price as three?"

"I think so."

"That's a bargain!"

"Jonie, you must be kidding!"

But Jonie wasn't. When the testing grades were released Gail sighed with relief over a high C. Jonie smiled over a D minus and was placed in bonehead English.

When their schedules were arranged Jonie decided that by working during mealtimes she could avoid wasting so much time standing in long dinner lines and going through checkout counters. This would give her more free time for study and other activites.

So she applied for and was hired to work in the cafeteria to supply the deck with fruit for breakfast and salads and desserts for dinner and supper. The only problem was that she felt she was forever running, trying to make it across campus in time to meet her after-meal appointments.

No matter how dark the morning might be, Jonie always awakened by an inner alarm clock and would slip quietly out of bed before 6:00 A.M. After a short devotion she took a quick, cold shower, toweled briskly, and slipped into a green-and-white uniform. Then she quickly brushed her hair and fairly flew down three flights of stairs, over the damp grass, and through the back door of the kitchen. She felt exhilarated hurrying through the brisk morning air, watching the Blue Mountains appear in the dawn, and catching the first notes of the meadowlark.

In the kitchen the steam would be rising from the large kettles of hot cereal and the stewed fruit for toast. Eggs would be spattering on the griddle, and the boys in tall white caps would be flipping pancakes. Wide-awake, Jonie took her place behind the counter with a glowing complexion and an easy smile for the many still-sleepy students filing through.

Jonie's first class was life and teachings of Christ. The alert white-haired gentleman standing behind the desk watched the new students as they came through the door and found seats. He knew the types—there were the studious few who quickly took places on the front row, several fun-loving young men who went noisily to the rear, a scattering of couples, a number of shy "loners" tucked in the corners, and a slender, dark-haired girl who found a place near the middle.

Elder Jenton, a small man behind thick glasses, took note of Jonie. Something in her manner captured his attention from the moment she entered the room. From her near-center seat she studied him intently, as though trying to anticipate his teaching ability. He met the serious, widely spaced eyes with a slight smile, nodding as he picked up the roll book. The room quieted as he called off the forty-odd names assigned to the Tuesday-Thursday seven-thirty section of life and teachings of Christ.

As the term progressed, Jonie found herself looking forward to this period with delight. At first, she drank in Elder Jenton's instruction while participating only a little, but after the first few classes, she could not suppress her thought-provoking questions that some-times challenged the would-be skeptics in the class-

room. It was only after stimulating discussion or
rousing debate that Elder Jenton satisfied his students
with clear-cut Biblical answers so readily available
from his mental storehouse of Bible texts. Life and
teachings was a class that sometimes left Jonie
searching for more answers on her own, but whatever
the format of the day, she alway left the room feeling
that she had been spiritually fed.

Bonehead English was another matter. The red
marks scattered generously throughout Jonie's compo-
sitions were upsetting. She worked more diligently,
putting her best into her efforts, only to be discouraged
again by low marks.

One evening Jonie noticed an English paper on
Gail's desk. It wore a bright red A minus. That was
almost more than Jonie could take. "A minus!" she
sputtered. "And she hates to write!"

The door opened, and Gail entered, having just
arrived from the library. Jonie turned around quickly,
and Gail's smile faded as she saw the perplexity on her
roommate's face.

Jonie opened her mouth, then pursed her lips.

"Well," Gail said, "should I prepare to be hung at
dawn?"

"What makes you ask that?"

"It's obvious you're bothered about something. I
suppose you've heard that I accepted a date with Chuck
for Saturday night. I wanted to tell you before someone
else did, honest."

Jonie sat down slowly, feeling strange in the pit of
her stomach. "No, Gail, I hadn't heard."

"Since Dick and I are on the outs again and you and
Chuck aren't a thing anymore, well, it just sort of
happened. He's been helping me in chem lab, and, well,
you know." Gail shrugged her shoulders in an attempt

at nonchalance. But she looked troubled.

Jonie nodded.

"But if you didn't know," Gail continued, "what was the matter when I walked in?"

"Not much, I guess. Just can't seem to make decent grades in English." Jonie was glad to change the subject. "I noticed that you're doing OK, though."

"I assure you it's not my style, Jonie. That lucky A is an old theme you helped me write last year. Saving it and redoing it happened to pay off. You should have saved yours."

"But that's like embroidering the second pillow-case," Jonie exclaimed.

"What do you mean?"

"Well, you don't have a choice of colors, there's no anticipation and nothing is new. It's boring, boring, boring."

"No, it's not, Jonie. It's easier. Anyway, I don't have your imagination. I'd just as soon do something over with no fuss. I can't see why you should be having problems, though, when you love writing so much. Of course, we do have two very different teachers. You should be in our class. Mr. Grange is a doll. At least, my style gets by him."

"Maybe that's my problem, my style. It sure doesn't make it with Miss Hammond."

The subject of Chuck's and Gail's date didn't come up again, but it hung in the air between the girls.

The following day Miss Hammond asked Jonie to meet with her after class to make arrangements for some special help. Jonie nodded, but felt her face flush in embarrassment. I guess I really do belong in bonehead English, after all, she thought. An appointment was made for three o'clock, then Jonie hurried to her next class.

Dr. Pratt smiled as she entered, almost late. Now this is one class I can relate to, she thought. Maybe I should teach speech. I've always believed that speaking in front of people should begin when one is still young. Besides, I get my best grades in speech. Could be I just like to talk. She smiled to herself.

At three o'clock Jonie entered the office of the dreaded Miss Hammond. She sat down and nervously waited while the woman behind the desk opened a folder and took out a composition. She frowned as she laid it before Jonie.

"Miss Owens, you seem to have trouble with both spelling and grammar. You constantly change tenses. This paper has too many mistakes to warrant a grade at all."

Sudden, hot tears stung Jonie's eyes, and she swallowed hard.

"Do you recognize that these are mistakes?"

Jonie peered at the paper and nodded her head slowly. A tear splashed on one of the ink checks, leaving a red blur.

Miss Hammond looked quickly at Jonie, and her face softened at the sight of the girl's misery. "Now, I am here to help you," she said.

"I—I guess maybe I've been too careless. I get carried away with what I'm thinking. My hand can hardly keep up with my thoughts, and I guess that's why some of my words get abbreviated, and I can see that I neglect to keep my tenses in order." Jonie spoke bravely, but inwardly she despaired. She doesn't say anything about the story. I guess I'll never be a writer, she thought.

"Now, my dear, if you realize your mistakes and work with more care, I'm sure your grades will improve." Miss Hammond paused, watching the girl, who sat quiet and pale before her. "Perhaps you have a problem that you'd like to share?"

"Thank you, I think I'm tired, that's all." The real problem was too close to Jonie's heart.

"If you wish to do this paper over I will make allowances this time."

"Thank you," Jonie answered, only too anxious to leave. She arose and started for the door.

"Just a moment, Miss Owens," Miss Hammond said, "I was wondering what your major is?"

Jonie hesitated, then replied quietly, "English."

"English! You wish to teach English?"

"I want to be a writer."

"A write——" Miss Hammond never finished the word.

"Yes," said Jonie, "a writer." Her voice was suddenly very positive. "It may take me till I'm 40, but I'll get there." She shut the door, leaving Miss Hammond slowly shaking her head.

What? No Date?

"THAT WENDY is absolutely a doll. She's just IT. She wears that soft white sweater and with those huge eyes she looks like a Persian kitten, all soft and cuddly—and every night I have to meet her in the bathroom." Jonie laid down her toothbrush and hung up her towel.

"So?" Gail said quizzically, laying aside her secretarial science books and watching Jonie kick off her slippers.

"Well, she always asks the same question." Jonie's voice raised two notes as she mimicked Wendy. " 'Have you been dated yet?' "

Gail fought back a giggle.

"Just 'cause she gets any guy she wants, she can rub it in."

"Well, she is a sophomore and she knows absolutely everybody," Gail replied.

"I doubt that it was any different for her this time last year when she was a freshman. All she has to do is look at a boy, and every night I'm spitting toothpaste and grunting 'un-unh' to her 'Any luck yet?'

"And then she says, 'Don't worry. You'll probably get one for the Amateur Hour!' " Jonie's voice was high soprano again.

Gail turned back her covers, trying hard not to laugh

at her roommate's ill humor. "Maybe she really is concerned, Jonie, and wants to be helpful."

Jonie wasn't sure.

"We've only been here two weeks," Gail said, "and a lot of kids aren't dating yet."

"You are!" Jonie's answer was too quick.

"Oh," said Gail, quietly. "That's bothering you."

"Of course not," Jonie snapped. "I don't care at all."

"Yes, you do care, Jonie. But if you do, why don't you go back to Chuck?"

"You know I can't do that. Besides, that would really look like I just couldn't get a date."

"Oh, that's ridiculous!"

"Is it? Just about every girl on this hall except you-know-who has a date for the Amateur Hour, and it's still two weeks away."

"You'll have one."

"I doubt it," grumbled Jonie, turning out the light.

Among the freshmen, the Amateur Hour became the biggest topic of conversation. For many, it was the beginning of college dating and a matter of status on both sides of the campus. Dinner lines buzzed with information and conjecture as to who was going with whom, who was taken, and who was left.

As the week dragged on, Jonie became more and more self-conscious. She changed her schedule so as to avoid bathroom encounters with Wendy. Then, during study period on Thursday night, the monitor tapped on the door, and Jonie was informed that she had a telephone call in the lobby.

She hurried down the three flights of stairs. When she returned, Gail looked expectant. "Who is he?" she asked.

"He! It was a *she*. Some senior girl wanting me to give the mission reading for Sabbath school. I'm glad

Wendy didn't see me. I can just hear her," and Jonie squeaked, "'What, no date *yet!*'"

Gail was quiet for a few moments, feeling Jonie's disappointment. Then she suggested brightly, "Why don't you begin studying in the library at night? Lots of kids get acquainted there."

"In the library?" Jonie looked at her roommate. "You mean people actually get dated in a stuffy old library?"

"Why not? It's as good as any place."

"But you can't even talk in a library."

"Who needs to talk?" Gail laughed.

Jonie spent Friday afternoon preparing the mission story. She wanted it to be different, so she rewrote it in the form of poetry.

Public speaking had never been particularly difficult for Jonie, but in the large auditorium before her peers and professors it was quite another story. As the song service ended, the Sabbath school officers and their assistants for the morning filed onto the platform, and Jonie felt her knees tremble slightly as they faced the front and sat down.

The special music was a quartet of four young men, who came in from the opposite side of the platform. As Jonie looked up, her eyes met the light gray ones of the dark-haired second tenor. The beautiful rendition of "Lift Up the Trumpet" relaxed Jonie, and when the number was finished and they turned to leave, another glance in Jonie's direction by that same young man left her wondering. Then her name was announced, and she walked forward to stand before the sea of faces. She offered a silent prayer for help as she began her piece.

"In the noonday's heat on thirsty land, sun-parched
    Army troops gathered gear, fell into order, then
    marched.
Artillery sounded, leaving no echo in its haste

As the sound was continuous and smoke filled the
waste."

Jonie's voice grew stronger as she felt the full
attention of her audience. Many of the men and a few of
the women sitting before her were war veterans. Her
words, spoken against a background of distant rum-
bling thunder and the sound of early fall rains blowing
against the windows awoke in the mind of each former
soldier scenes repressed but not forgotten. In the
auditorium there was not a sound save the clear voice of
the girl behind the microphone.

"Where the gazelle once wandered and sunset
silhouetted the giraffe,
Where freely roamed the pride and winds carried the
hyenas' laugh,
Now strewn with bodies bleeding after the vulture
has long flown,
And men fight the battle of pain, collectively, yet
alone.
Back in a Congo mission whistling bullets riddle the
walls.
On the compound, no children singing, no jungle bird
calls.
In the crossfire of bazookas and *whoom* of large
shells,
Behind a temporary fortress, a missionary wonders,
'Will they live to tell
Once again the love of Jesus, the story of peace on
earth?
Will there be sweet singing in the chapel or a
schoolyard ringing with mirth?'
Water and supplies are dwindling, the roof is partly
gone.
They make preparation to escape before the coming
dawn.

Silently, with few possessions, they each make their
  way
To the old supply truck that has seen a better day.
There are anxious moments of agony when the
  engine doesn't start.
Then, during a noisy burst of mortar, there's a shiver
  in the cart.
Miraculously quiet and without light, they drive a
  circuitous route
Through lonely, isolated roads, but never once with a
  doubt
That angels are guiding on this evacuation night.
The airstrip will be found in the dawning light.
There, ahead, they see the planes; soon they will be
  soaring.
But strict orders against takeoff, a result of all the
  warring
Leave them once again to ponder what God would
  have them do.
With a prayer, they prepare as if they already knew
That the way will open, though there be foxholes all
  around,
And the airport runway is through very dangerous
  ground.
Permission is finally given. They speed past the
  dugouts,
Thankful for a momentary cease fire and this chance
  to reroute.
Seeking cover in the clouds, the blue Cessna lifts to
  the sky.
With relief, a mother holds her children and stifles a
  cry.
The young father at the throttle looks down with
  concern,
'Hold your fire, you trigger-happy fools, this plane

aims to return!' "

Jonie paused, studied her audience for a second or two, then continued.

"We admire their courage momentarily, then soon forget
What it takes to spread the gospel. May we someday not regret
That while many do their work and live in conditions of fear,
We have not neglected in giving, because we really care."

As Jonie seated herself she glanced up to discover Miss Hammond in the side section of the balcony just above her. She was leaning slightly forward and appeared thoughtful.

"Oh, no," Jonie breathed. "I hope I got my tenses all straight."

Jonie spent most of Sunday doing extra work in the cafeteria. She studied some in the afternoon and saved her psychology to work on in the library. Judy, from the next room, joined her when she left that evening. "I would have started going to the library sooner if I'd known that you study over there," Jonie told her. Jonie was attracted to this neighbor and fascinated by her roommate, Alyce.

"I've only gone twice," Judy told her. "I don't care much about going alone either. Your roommate goes quite often. Don't you run around with her much?"

"Some, but not altogether. We love each other dearly or we wouldn't have spent so many years as roommates. But we do live independently of each other, too. We choose some friends separately and share others. We go our separate ways and then have more to share with each other when we are alone. We enjoy our relationship the way it is without being tied to each other."

"I guess Alyce and I are as different as night and day," Judy said. "That's why I find her very interesting. Now, what did you bring to study? Not much, it appears," Judy answered herself.

"That's right. Why?"

"Well, I don't have much to do either, and there's a concert at Columbia Auditorium at eight that I would like to hear. Alyce is playing the cello."

"Well, let's go. I just have psych, and that won't take me till eight." The girls entered the library and were walking briskly away again by seven-forty-five. It was a beautiful night, starlit, and fragrant with autumn. Sharing amusing girl talk and enjoying each other's company, they joined the crowd in Columbia Auditorium and found places in the middle section of the front, where Judy could watch her roommate perform.

"I'm very partial to strings," Jonie said, watching the group warm up. "My father and grandfather both play violins."

"I'm taking piano," Judy told her. "Look, Jonie, see that blond fellow behind Alyce. That's the one who asked me to the Amateur Hour."

Jonie nodded. "Ummm. Did you know him before?" she whispered to Judy, as the conductor took his place.

"Never. Just met him in European-civilization class. He's from Auburn."

Jonie nodded again, then settled back comfortably, listening to the rising and falling of the music. It reminded her of ocean waves quietly slipping into shore. Then came the thundering of drums, the crash of cymbals, lightning, waves pounding rocks, and from somewhere the call of a gull. The music spoke, and Jonie followed, her mind on a guided tour.

During intermission Jonie exclaimed about the blending of so many talents.

"That's very true," Judy agreed. "I'll bet the Amateur Hour will be great."

"No doubt."

"Do you have——?"

"Oh, Judy, not you too. I've been asked that question so often I feel just plain embarrassed."

"Jonie, I'm sorry," Judy said with dismay. "But, don't worry, you'll get a date." She hastened to add, "The guys just don't know you're available."

Jonie reached over and squeezed her hand. "Thanks for trying. It's really OK."

The music resumed, but Jonie's mind was preoccupied now, perplexed over her dateless situation. She had to admit it wasn't OK. She leaned back in her chair, looking far beyond the performers. *What's wrong with me, Father? Am I really so bad that nobody wants to take me out? If You are trying to teach me something, help me to know and accept, but if it's all right with You, Father, I'd like a date, too.*

Sitting upright again, she suddenly realized that she really didn't know whom she wanted a date with. Then a face flashed into her mind. *Please, Father, if it's OK, I'd like it to be that second tenor. Thank You.*

From then on, Jonie relaxed and enjoyed the music, her problem in good hands to be solved one way or another. After the concert Judy decided to wait for Alyce. Jonie smiled. "Any other attraction up there?"

"Well, maybe." Judy laughed.

"That's OK, but I'm going on back to the dorm. I've had a long day."

They parted, and Jonie was soon a part of the crowd. As she neared the back door, a tall, gray-eyed young man with several books under his arm stood watching her. As she glanced in his direction, he fell in beside her.

"Would you mind if I walk you to the dorm?" he

asked. Jonie liked his voice immediately.

"I'd like that," she answered, almost shyly.

"You're Joan Owens."

"Jonie to most, but how did you know?"

"You did a super job of the mission reading yesterday, and I remember your name."

"Well, you did a super job with the special music, and I remember your name—Stan Reeves.

They both laughed.

"What's your major, Stan?"

"Biology. I'm taking premed. What's yours?"

"I hate to tell you."

"Why?"

"It's English."

"Oh. Whose class are you in?"

"That's what I hate to tell you. I'm in bonehead."

"Bonehead? And you want to major in English?"

"Well, I thought I was doing myself a favor by getting into Miss Hammond's class. I want to be a writer, but she isn't very encouraging."

Stan turned toward her. "Tell me one thing."

"Sure."

"Did you write that mission reading?"

She hesitated, then nodded.

"Then don't use the future tense, 'going to be.' Jonie, you *are* a writer." Stan's voice was very positive.

Jonie smiled in appreciation. She couldn't have received a nicer compliment. They were almost to the dorm.

"What are you doing Saturday night?" His voice was casual.

Jonie was still relishing the compliment. "Let's see, next Saturday night. What's going on?"

Stan looked at her in surprise. "The Amateur Hour!" he exclaimed.

"Oh, that's right!" Jonie was glad it was dark, for her face was suddenly hot.

"Would you go with me?" he asked.

"I'd love to." She was smiling again.

They had reached the dorm. Jonie thanked Stan and fled inside. She raced up three flights of stairs and flung open the door to her dark room where Gail was sleeping soundly.

"Wake up, Gail! Wake up!" Jonie shook the bed.

Gail mumbled something inaudible, turned on her back and began breathing heavily again.

"I've got a date, Gail, I've got a date!"

Gail suddenly sat upright. "A date!" She hopped out of bed and spun Jonie in a little circle on the soft rug in the still-dark room. They fell on the bed, laughing.

"Oh, Jonie, I've been praying."

"Me too," Jonie murmured. "I was getting worried."

"But, tell me, do you like him?"

"Roommate, he's exactly what I ordered."

The next evening Jonie chanced to meet Wendy at the washbasins again. With her sweet, cheerful concern, Wendy inquired, "Have you been dated for the Amateur Hour yet?" Jonie's mouth was full of paste, and she didn't answer. "I know someone I ought to introduce you to, a really nice guy." Jonie looked up. This girl was for real, after all.

"Thank you, Wendy, but I have a date."

"You do! Who is it?"

"Stan Reeves."

Wendy's mouth dropped open. "Stan Reeves! Why, he's a confirmed bachelor," she gasped. "I've been trying for a date with him for ages."

Jonie gathered her toilet articles and left, feeling suddenly just a little smug, knowing that Wendy was still watching her as she walked out the door. No doubt she wonders how I did it. I guess I didn't. God did, she reminded herself.

Saturday night glistened with raindrops, wet sidewalks, and happy couples under dripping umbrellas. Alyce came into Jonie's room to inspect herself in the full-length mirror. Her blond hair was shining, and her large eyes were lightly made up, accenting their width. Her face was very carefully put on with only a hint of pink, as subtle as her manner. She wore a long black taffeta skirt and white blouse. In her high-heeled shoes she stood close to six feet tall.

"I have a very special date with an upperclassman," Alyce stated to Jonie and Gail, who were watching with interest. "I've been after this one since I saw him the first week of school. So I want to be sure I am dressed simply enough so that he notices me and not my clothes."

Gail got off the bed and walked barefoot over to stand beside Alyce. She looked her over from head to toe with exaggerated slowness. "It's just too much, just too much," she said, teasing. "Do you think he will notice her, Jonie?"

Jonie smiled at Gail's nonsense. Alyce ignored her.

"You do look beautiful," Jonie said sincerely.

"Yes, but it's very difficult being beautiful. A man once told my mother that such a beautiful child can only bring pain and receive pain."

The door flew open, and Judy rushed in. "Hurry, Alyce, he's here, and look, this came for you." Alyce took another deliberate turn before the mirror, raised her skirt and inspected her stockings, then took the box from Judy.

Very carefully, she opened the lid and closed it again. "Violets. That's what I call perfect taste. He's evidently noticed the color of my eyes. I'll let him pin them on. I'd say he's already impressed," and she walked regally out the door. Judy followed.

"Not half as impressed as she is, I bet," Gail said, doing a little half turn on her tiptoes in front of the mirror, lifting up the corner of her slip and looking at her legs.

"Gail, that doesn't even sound like you." Jonie laughed. "She's just incredibly honest."

"And stuck on herself," Gail added.

Jonie had her head in the closet trying to decide what to wear. She had changed her mind several times that week. "O that I could look so elegant!" she moaned.

"Just wear your wine velvet suit and white satin blouse and you will," her roommate said.

Jonie slipped the suit from its hanger and began to dress, keeping a careful eye on the clock. Then came the announcement that her date had arrived, and she felt butterflies take over in her stomach. Before leaving, she turned to Gail, who was tying the belt of her blue dress. "Have a really great time tonight, roommate. And I truly mean that."

"Jonie, any date with Chuck is one long evening of me talking about Dick, and Chuck talking about you. He still cares, you know!"

"So do I," Jonie answered. "But I'm not going to let it spoil college for me."

In the boys' dorm quite another scene had taken place. Chuck had just entered his room to find his roommate gone and their friend Dick's belongings scattered all over the room. His Columbia Academy letterman sweater lay on the floor, a notebook and papers were scattered across the bed. "Why can't that guy remember to take his belongings to his own room?"

Chuck muttered, his face flushing.

Pete, a deep bass, entered, dressed in his quartet suit. "Good luck tonight, roommate," Chuck greeted him. "You guys ought to be a smash."

There was a tap on the door, and Pete shouted, "Come in," to Stan Reeves, who had come with some last-minute instructions regarding the quartet. Chuck was introduced to Stan, who kept glancing beyond him at a sixteen-by-twenty-four-inch portrait of Jonie that dominated the room. There were two other poses of the girl on the desk.

"She your girl?" Stan asked.

"Was," Chuck muttered.

"Oh. I wondered. I asked her to the Amateur Hour. Pete, are you ready? We're going to have to make tracks if we're going to run through our number before picking up dates."

"I'm coming. I'm coming."

The door clicked behind them, and Chuck snatched up the notebook from the bed and flung it out the window with a vengeance. The sweater followed, then the pants and shirt.

Five minutes later good-natured Dick entered unannounced and asked, "You heard about Jonie's date?"

"I heard, I saw, I met, and if you don't keep your junk out of here, we'll wipe our feet on it."

"All right, all right. OK, where's my stuff?"

"Four flights down," Chuck growled, pointing out the window.

The downstairs lobby of the girls' residence hall was filled with young men, each looking expectantly toward the stairs. The descending girls were indeed lovely and worth waiting for.

Jonie suddenly felt nervous before all those scrutinizing male eyes. Then she realized that most of the men were as concerned as she was, and she smiled warmly at Stan as he made his way toward her.

Together they went out the door. He placed his arm at her convenience and she slipped her hand through as they descended the steps.

"They're expecting such a crowd tonight that the program will be given in both Columbia Auditorium and the library chapel. Since the quartet is singing in the two places, it was better to get seats at the library. We're near the first, so as soon as we're through, we'll leave Columbia and finish out the program at the library. I hope you don't mind."

"Not at all. That just makes it more exciting."

Stan looked relieved, and the evening promised to be a success.

Jonie met the other members of the quartet and their dates and shared the excitement of seeing the boys win first place in their section in both buildings. When she returned to her room she knew she would long remember that evening. The time on her knees before retiring was not without special gratitude to God for taking care of even the trifles in life that at times seem to be of great importance to a young girl.

Speech Countdown

JONIE OPENED her mailbox and found a slip requesting her presence in the registrar's office. She went there directly after attending introduction to speech class.

The registrar sorted through some cards and said, "Miss Owens, you added three speech classes to your curriculum, and this third one is an upper-division course."

"Isn't that all right?" Jonie wanted to know.

"No. It's not permissible for a lower-division student to take an upper-division class. You must fill the prerequisite requirements first. How is it that you are taking this many speech classes, anyway?"

"Shortly after school started I decided to change my major from English to speech and I signed up for all the classes I could work in."

"Well, I'm afraid you'll have to drop this one."

"But I'm doing fine in that class. My grades are high."

"It still isn't allowed, Jonie."

"I have more than a month invested in it already." Jonie's concern was showing.

"Perhaps we can arrange for a refund since this wasn't caught sooner."

"You can't refund the time and effort spent," Jonie

persisted, keeping her voice and expression calm.

The woman looked exasperated. "I'm sorry. There is nothing I can do."

Turning toward the door, Jonie breathed, "Father, please help me." Suddenly she turned back. "How many students do you have to have in order to offer a class?"

"Seven."

"Then I guess you'll have to discontinue that class."

"Why?" the woman looked puzzled.

"Because if I withdraw there will be only six enrolled."

The registrar hesitated, studying the situation. "Well, I suppose we could call a special meeting on this."

"Please do. If I'm getting good grades and I do all the work, couldn't I get lower-division credit for my upper-division work?"

"We will give it some consideration and notify you."

Jonie walked from the room thankful that she had been impressed to ask a question that had not occurred to her before.

Speech classes were fun. The more she learned the more convinced she was that teaching speech would be an ideal way to challenge young people into greater and more effective witnessing. She was happy when the registrar notified her that she would be allowed to continue with her third class.

Dr. Pratt and Mrs. Tallman announced that all two hundred students taking speech in their classes should prepare to talk for five to seven minutes on temperance in any form. Notes were not permissible, and since it was to be a contest, there would be elimination trials in the classrooms. The twenty-five best speeches would be presented before a panel of speech majors. Ten chosen from that group would speak before a board of professors. The five chosen from the semifinals would

speak in Columbia Auditorium before the student body
and visitors, including the mayor of Walla Walla. "Now,
you may drop out after the preliminary trials should you
be chosen from the original two hundred, but we hope
you will continue," they were informed.

Jonie sighed. "You'd really have to be good to go that
far," she whispered to the young man sitting beside her.

"You could do it," he whispered back.

"No, thanks. You know how many speech classes I'm
in? They're going to get sick of me."

Jonie went home for Thanksgiving. She had gained
fourteen pounds and was in radiant good health. Her
parents and friends raved at the improvement in her
appearance. "College is the best thing that's happened
to you," her mother exclaimed.

"Could it be the change of climate up there?" her
father asked.

"Probably all those treats at the Shake Shop with the
boys," her brother teased.

"Some things never change around here—namely
him," Jonie retorted.

"Could be he's right. How about it, honey?" her
father asked.

"Maybe now and then, but if I've gained it's because
I'm so busy that when I finally do eat I'm starved.
College is all so interesting and exciting, Daddy. I love
Bible and psych, but, well, I'll have to admit that I'm not
that thrilled with English."

"That's unusual," her mother said.

"I know, but I love art and speech. Oh, yes, I have a
lot of work to do on a special talk I'm preparing for a
contest."

"Contest?" her brother asked. "Are you going to
win?"

"Of course not, silly. There are two hundred students

preparing for it, and a lot of them are theology majors, and I mean *really* talented." She proceeded to give the particulars.

"Well, I'll bet on you, Sis," her brother said confidently. "You'll make it to the finals. I know you will."

Jonie laughed and shook her head. "Don't get carried away. The competition is pretty stiff."

Her mother smiled at her and said, "Well, if you should make it to the finals, Jonie, we are going to come up to hear you. When you were at Columbia Academy we were in Arizona and I missed everything you did except your graduation. I don't intend to miss anything as exciting as the finals of a speech contest, if you should be in it."

"Really, Mother? Now I have to make it to the finals."

"You can do it," her father assured her.

"Why not?" Jimmy said. "Especially with your gift of gab."

"I can sure tell I'm home again," Jonie said, smiling at her family.

Vacation passed much too swiftly, yet Jonie could hardly wait to get back on campus and do some research at the college library. She was determined now to win, impossible though it seemed. She left home very early Sunday morning and arrived on campus before noon. She unpacked and looked forward to an afternoon and evening of hard work.

Jonie had dated a number of fellows since Amateur Hour, but occasionally she and Stan met in the library to study. She secretly admired him and hoped he might be there tonight.

At dinner, a junior girl who was active in many extracurricular activities sat down with Jonie and

invited her to a party that evening. Jonie was attracted
to her warm, easygoing manner. *I always liked people
with red hair,* she thought, remembering Chuck's
coppery thatch. *They're the ones it's hard for me to say
No to, and I really haven't time for a party.*

"Jonie, would you consider a blind date with a
senior?" And when Jonie shook her head negatively, the
charming girl persisted, "Why not?"

"They usually want to get married sooner than I do. I
mean, why risk not finishing college?"

Her new friend laughed.

"You wouldn't consider it at all? I know one who's
very interested in you."

"Sorry, but not tonight anyway."

Jonie hurried to the library after dinner and gave
the books her best. By five o'clock she was mentally
exhausted. Supper was a welcome relief.

"Say, you look tired from all that study."

Jonie looked up to see her friend from dinner.

"Sure you wouldn't like to take a break and go to that
party? It would do you good, and I've got another blind
date for you. This one isn't a senior."

Jonie laughed. "OK, you win. Where and when?"

Arrangements were made, and Jonie was escorted
by a sandy-haired junior to a party at a young married
couple's house. They played table games, and the
evening was a relaxing change from a day of mental
pressures. Jonie made an effort to enjoy Rodney. She
tried to overlook his perpetual grin and nervous BO. But
as the evening progressed, the room became close and
warm, and Jonie felt she would suffocate in her own
politeness.

It was a welcome suggestion by the hostess that the
girls line up on the front porch where their escorts
blindfolded them and tied bibs around their necks. From

a table of condiments and other flavorings, they were given a sample taste. Jonie swallowed a pinch of this, a drop of that, guessing good-naturedly. She was glad to be outdoors even though it was chilly. Suddenly, a whole tablespoon of a dry substance was emptied down her throat. She swallowed hard, gagged, and sputtered. Pulling off the blindfold, she looked up at the perpetual grin. Then she leaned over the porch rail, choking and spitting. Her eyes watered as the penetrating taste of garlic powder stabbed her taste buds. No amount of water took the flavor away. Jonie was turned off on blind dates forever. And during the following week, Rodney seemed to turn up around every corner, wearing his cheerful grin, and every time she politely said Hello, she tasted garlic.

Jonie's efforts at the library had paid off. In the next few days she gave her speech in three different classes and made it into a group of twenty-five chosen by classroom voting. Judy, who was in one of the speech classes but had no desire to do any more than satisfy the first requirement, took great interest in Jonie's determination and progress.

"Have you any idea who's on that semifinal panel of senior-speech-major judges?" Jonie asked as the two girls shared an umbrella beneath the dripping eaves on the way from class.

"Some older students, two of them returned vets, I think," Judy responded.

"I hope they're fair. I mean, it just might be sort of easy to select your best friend when having to choose."

"Oh, Jonie, I'm sure they will try to make an honest evaluation."

"Maybe I'd be better off if they didn't."

"You don't want to win."

"Oh, yes, I do. You don't know how much it would

really delight my folks to be able to come and see me do
something. My mother always felt cheated because I
went to academy so far away from her and she missed
out on so much."

"If it is really important, we'll just pray about it,"
Judy told her.

"I have, and the one answer I get is practice, practice,
practice—so I do—thirty times a day."

"Thirty!"

"That's right. I can say it in my sleep with no
mistakes. I'm afraid it's becoming mechanical. I'll really
have to concentrate in order to have any expression. I'm
becoming a robot at it"

Judy laughed."A little stage fright will probably
take care of that."

"And you are probably so right," Jonie answered.

Caught up with her new major and its requirements,
Jonie was beginning to let her other classes slip a little.
One morning Elder Jenton detained her on the way out
of life and teachings. "Miss Owens, could you stop by my
office sometime this afternoon?"

"Certainly," she replied, but not without concern.

When she entered his office after dinner, Elder
Jenton smiled and rose from behind the large desk to
shake her hand.

"This is the first time you have been here."

"Yes." Jonie hesitated, then asked, "Are my grades
slipping?"

"No, no, no. I was assigned as your advisor and I'm
sorry I have not made your acquaintance sooner except
in the classroom. You have been a good student, a most
challenging one, in fact. Sit down, sit down."

Jonie looked relieved and took a chair. Elder Jenton
sat down and peered over his small glasses, then
removed them and continued to study her from across

the desk. This girl did not appear to be uncomfortable in his presence, but seemed to be studying him with a concentration equal to his own.

"Well, young lady, tell me something of yourself. What is it like to be Jonie Owens?"

She smiled. "I am from Portland, Oregon, a Columbia Academy graduate. I like horses, skiing, oil painting, and good books when I have time to read them. I like to cook, climb mountains, and ice skate. Most of all, I enjoy writing. My mother is very musical. She usually wakes us in the morning by playing beautiful music on the piano. To me, putting words together so that they flow smoothly or have a certain rhythym is somewhat like beautiful music."

The man nodded, leaning back in his chair. "Do you like college?"

"Oh, very much, but it's hard to keep up sometimes."

"What is your major?"

"Speech."

"Speech!" he came forward suddenly.

"Yes."

"What would a girl like you ever do with speech? That's mostly a class for theology majors."

"I don't see why." Jonie stiffened. She had always hated being told anything was mostly for boys. "I think impromptu speaking ought to be taught on the secondary level or even sooner so that youngsters will become accustomed to thinking on their feet. Then, maybe someday there won't be so many people who just sit in their pews on Sabbath because they think they would die of fright if they were to take part in the program."

He chuckled at her long speech. "Well, if you like teaching, maybe education should be your major, or even English." Jonie sat quietly. Elder Jenton was refusing to see her point. "So far," he continued. "Speech is not being taught in many of our academies, so you could be wasting your time. It really is a course prepared for men."

"And I hope to see that changed," Jonie countered.

"Perhaps. You have a point." He could see she had a great deal of determination in her makeup. "Well, Miss Owens, I hadn't planned to detain you for long. I'm here for counseling should you need me. I've looked forward to getting better acquainted with you since the first day of classes. In fact, I particularly noticed you that first day. When you walked in and took your place I said, 'Now there is a girl with inborn culture.'"

"Why, thank you," Jonie said, rising with the professor to shake hands and leave. When she went to her room she got out the dictionary and looked up the word *culture,* trying to understand what the gentleman's compliment was all about.

Unexpected Assistance

THE AFTERNOON speech-practice session was the next thing on her agenda, and after it was over, Jonie went to work. As she left the cafeteria a young man coming down the walk fell in step with her.

"Good evening, Jonie."

"Hello, Tom." She recognized him as one of the speech majors who had judged the competition.

"May I offer you some assistance and maybe a few pointers in the coming weeks?"

"Assistance?" she questioned, looking at this man who was virtually a stranger. What was he talking about?

"You're surprised? Oh, of course! You haven't seen the semifinal list. It's posted outside the speech office. Congratulations on being one of the winners."

"Really? I made it!" Jonie beamed and sent a silent prayer of thanks heavenward.

"That's right. Excuse my assumption that you knew. There were eight men and two women selected. I thought you might be interested in using the mike for practice, and since I have a part-time job in the speech department, I can make some time for you."

"I'd appreciate that," Jonie answered gratefully.

"I would walk you to the dorm, but my other job is

downtown at the radio station, and it's about time to
deliver the evening news. So if you like, stop by the
speech department at four o'clock tomorrow afternoon.
I'll be watching for you." He turned and walked away.
He was whistling.

Jonie walked thoughtfully to her room, curiously
intrigued. She wondered about this self-assured young
man, a returned veteran, with Nordic good looks.

Linda and Beth, Jonie's grade-school friends who
lived below her, walked into her room a few minutes
later and found her standing on a chair reciting her
number.

"That explains it," Linda laughed.

"Explains what?" Jonie asked, jumping off the chair.

"The noise we hear every so often," Beth said. "The
first few times we wondered whether you had fallen."

"No, I'm just getting used to the platform feeling."

"Well, good luck. When are the finals?" this from
Linda.

"Monday night, and I won't have any chance to
practice Sunday, because I'll be skiing all day."

Linda put her fingers on Jonie's shoulders and began
massaging the tense muscles.

"Oh, Linda, how I will always remember and
appreciate you!" Jonie lay down on her bed, and Linda
continued the massage up and down her back until all
the tension was gone. "Ummmm, that feels so good. I
remember once when our grade-school teacher said to
me, 'Jonie, there is one thing you know how to do well,
and that is to pick a good friend. Linda is the kind of
friend that will fit in any niche and always wear well.'"

Beth nodded in agreement, and Linda blushed and
smiled with pleasure.

Jonie slept much easier that night after the rubdown
and the encouragement of her childhood friends. By

afternoon she felt ready and almost eager to face the microphone and the willing assistance of Tom, who was waiting for her in the speech department. Upon her arrival, he turned off the machine he was testing and disappeared behind a curtain, calling for her to follow. They emerged backstage on the platform at the other end of the department.

Tom set the mike up and showed Jonie how to use it. She recited a few lines and he said, "Come with me." Again she followed, this time to Columbia Auditorium. "Now," he instructed, "you will stand middle stage before the mike. There will be no podium and you are not allowed notes."

"But, Tom, what's this all about? I haven't won the assurance that this opportunity is mine yet."

"You will. Trust me."

Jonie swallowed, watching his brisk movement as he set up the mike. "I might lose, you know, and then I'd hate to think I had wasted so much of your time," she said.

"I don't consider you a waste of time, Jonie. Believe me, you do have a great talent."

"Thank you, but so do some of the others I'm up against."

"Jonie, all you need is more self-confidence."

"Perhaps, but you must admit I've got *some* competition."

"I'm not denying that, but you have *me* to coach you and plenty of time to make perfection."

For a moment Jonie was silent as she faced him on the empty stage. "I appreciate all your efforts, Tom. I do feel very fortunate. I hope I'm not a disappointment"

"Never." He turned and smiled at her. "Now, come and see how this mike is for height." After a few minor adjustments, he left the platform and took his place in the middle of the empty auditorium and waited for her to speak. Jonie appeared small and vulnerable as she stood alone on the wide expanse of oak flooring framed by the deep-red curtains. She hesitated, inhibited by his presence.

"It's all right, Jonie." Because of the distance between them, it was necessary for Tom to raise his voice, but there was a touch of tenderness in his tone in contrast to his usual businesslike manner.

Jonie proceeded hesitantly, and almost immediately Tom interrupted. "Now start over and really emphasize that first line. Wake 'em up," he shouted, socking his fist into his palm as he walked forward. "If you're the last one to speak they may all be falling asleep by now."

Jonie laughed. "Not after Des gets done with them." She was finally loosening up and began again with the special sparkle her tutor was seeking. "Oh, no, the liquor problem does not affect *us!* Why, we're a group of people who do *not* drink!"

"Good, very good." He smiled up at her, his bass voice echoing against the walls.

Jonie continued, playing to the main floor, the front balcony, to the left and right footlights, the back and side balconies and, finally, to the man watching so intently in front of her.

"Bravo," he said, applauding loudly when she finished. "I don't think we can improve on that."

She smiled, feeling more confident.

"Now, if you do that well Monday night you'll be one of the judges' choices to speak here before the mayor and the rest of the town fathers next month, for sure."

"But the contents of my speech, Tom, what about that?" she said, with some doubt.

"Well, it's a little late now to rewrite and relearn. I wouldn't touch it. You made it with the student judges.

It compared well."

"Yet, I feel it lacks something."

"If it does, you make up for it, Jonie." He smiled reassuringly.

When Jonie woke up Sunday morning she felt miserable. Her back and head ached, and she knew she had no business going skiing, but she convinced herself that once on the slopes she would forget her problem. The day was snow-weather perfect. The hills and the crowd were just right for good skiing, and Stan was there. He made the day extra special for Jonie by skiing with her much of the time. But that night she crawled miserably into bed, and Monday morning she stayed there.

By evening, she felt better as she showered and dressed. The red wool top and winter-white swinging wool skirt had been favorites of Chuck. He had helped her shop after school once and selected this particular outfit. Let's hope it brings me good luck tonight, she thought, and she tied on a perky red-and-white scarf and fastened her belt.

Grabbing up her notebook with the speech neatly typed and underlined inside, she hurried to the administration building. All was a twitter in the speech office. Jonie laid aside her notebook after a hurried last-minute glance at her material. She drew a number from a hat which established the fact that she would be the fourth one to speak. Then she took her seat with the other finalists on the front row before the platform.

Jonie had heard most of the speeches before, but tonight each orator was at his best, more convincing, more polished, more alive. There was an electric tension in the air. Jonie glanced at the judges in the back of the room and noted that they were making careful notes. She shivered, yet her cheeks felt hot and flushed. Too soon it was her turn.

Before the small, friendly audience, Jonie lost her jitters. Elder Jenton was in the back peering over his glasses at her, and there was Tom, smiling his reassurance. She smiled back and began strongly with confidence, the way he had taught her. For several minutes she spoke with her usual animation. Then, oddly, she paused for a few moments, and when she continued, the words came more slowly and with effort.

Mrs. Tallman stood listening behind the curtain in the speech department. She turned to one of her assistants and whispered, "What's happened to Jonie? She suddenly lost all her sparkle."

On the platform, Jonie paused again, her face—so full of color only moments before—now very white. "I'm sorry," she said, "but I think I'm going to faint." She braced herself against the lectern, swayed slightly, then let go and walked crookedly toward the stairs. She took one step down and knew she'd never make the rest. Sinking slowly to the top step to sit for a moment, she suddenly blacked out and fell sideways to the floor.

There was an instant reaction in the room. Two young men on the front row sprang forward and carried her to an adjacent office. Tom ran from the room for water. When Jonie opened her eyes to the clucking concern of Mrs. Tallman, there were several others about, including Tom. She sat up. "Oh, dear! I didn't finish my speech!"

"Now, don't worry about that," her professor advised. "You need to be just one place and that's in your room resting."

"Oh, no!" Jonie's voice was alarmed. "I have to finish. I wasn't through. I don't know what happened. I just blacked out. I'm OK now."

Tom spoke firmly. "I'll take you to the dorm, Jonie."

"No, I am going back in there and finish."

Tom and Mrs. Tallman looked at each other for a moment. In the short silence, Jonie heard a barely distinguishable voice that floated back through the curtains. "That's Des. As soon as he's finished could I just try again?" She reached for her notebook and glanced in it.

"Are you sure you feel like it, Jonie?" Mrs. Tallman looked concerned.

"Oh, yes, I'm fine now."

When Jonie stepped through the curtains a few minutes later, the professors and students looked surprised, to say the least.

"I'm sorry for the interruption in my speech. I was ill today and perhaps should not have come tonight, but since I have begun, I would like, with your permission, to finish."

The judges nodded. She was still very pale, a little shaken and felt thankful there was not a great deal left to say. After her closing statement, she said, "Thank you for allowing me to continue." She left the stage, then walked down the hall past the speech department and hurried back to the dorm, alone.

Gail, Judy, Linda, Beth, and several others were studying in the parlor, waiting for Jonie's return. They all hurried into the hall when she arrived. "How'd you do?" "Tell us how it went." "Do you think you will be chosen?" "Have you won?" The girlish voices were sweet in their excitement.

Jonie stood quietly for a moment, watching her friends' eager faces. Even the dean was there, smiling expectantly, waiting for the answer. "Won? Not exactly. No chance of that!" Jonie's face mirrored dismay and disappointment.

Mrs. Spring stepped forward quickly and put her

hand on Jonie's shoulder, searching the girl's unhappy
face. "Whatever happened, Jonie?"

"Nothing, I just fainted in the middle of it all." A
little exclamation of dismay escaped the dean's lips.
Then she took Jonie's arm and walked upstairs with her
while the subdued girls looked wide-eyed at one
another.

Gail spoke. "I knew she shouldn't try to give that
speech tonight. But you know Jonie. Nothing would
have kept her down."

Soon after Jonie awoke in the morning, a silver tray
arrived from a catering service. It was spread with a
lovely breakfast garnished with a bouquet of pink and
white carnations and her hometown newspaper. She
didn't know what to make of it. "Even *The Oregonian,*
my own newspaper," she mused aloud.

Judy, who was monitoring on the first floor, had
delivered the tray. "If you are going to have boyfriends
like this," she said to the wondering girl, "do you have to
live up three flights of stairs in the most remote region of
the dorm?"

"But I don't have any boyfriends like this. I have no
idea!"

"Oh, Jonie, it's from Tom. Who else?"

"It must be, but why?"

"*Why?* I would think that's obvious."

"Yes, I suppose he feels sorry for me 'cause I really
blew it last night."

"That's not all he feels, I bet, and besides, last night
wasn't your fault."

Jonie leisurely enjoyed the fresh fruit and the rest of
the lovely meal, then perused the newspaper briefly
before falling asleep again.

She was roused at noon by a wild banging on her
door, and Judy rushed in.

"Sleepyhead, wake up! Wake up!"

Jonie opened her eyes trying to find her way out of a deep sleep and into reality.

"You won! You won! You really did it!"

"Judy, don't tease me like that. You know how disappointed I am. I don't even want to think about it."

"But, Jonie, you really did. I ran over to the ad building to get a book I left, and there were five names posted on the bulletin board and yours was one of them. Really, it was!" Judy paused, reading speechless disbelief on Jonie's face.

Then there were tears wanting to fall as Jonie sat up. "Oh, Judy, how could God be so good to me when I was such a flop?"

"Well, it couldn't have been all that bad," Judy laughed.

"Now my folks will come when I speak at Columbia Auditorium. They will be so pleased. Tom said I could make it. I wonder how he knew. I sure didn't."

"Well, we all prayed you would."

"How true," Jonie smiled, the tears still sparkling in her eyes.

The Art of Saying No

"JONIE, WHERE have you been?" Gail said, looking up quickly. Four girls sitting in the twin beds did the same as Jonie came through the door and shrugged off her long winter coat. She was wearing her gym shorts.

"I guess that should be obvious," Jonie said, pulling off her damp, icy tennis shoes.

"You've been in the gym all this time?" Judy asked.

"Well, not exactly. I was playing basketball. There was this fellow, Lew, who was trying to help me perfect a hook shot after we finished the game and, well, we went for some hot chocolate and got to talking. But why am I explaining all this? Study period hasn't started yet."

"But, Jonie, I thought we were going to get together before study period and figure out six congenial guys to invite to the Girls' Club banquet and then all sit together," Gail reminded her.

"I did find out that the tables were being set up for twelve," Trish added. She was a pretty blonde girl who lived across the hall.

"OK, what have we got?" Jonie looked from one girl to the next, contemplating their dates—Judy with Rick from Auburn; Trish with Dan, from Takoma Academy; Beth with Gale, Columbia; Linda and—— "Linda, are you going to ask that guy who sits next to you in history?

I don't know his name."

"Yes, if you mean the one from Shenandoah Valley."

"So that leaves you, Gail," Jonie said, looking at her roommate.

"I'm going to ask Ted."

"Ted?" Trish asked.

"Yes, the fellow with the crippled arm from San Francisco."

Trish nodded. "The one who's been walking you everywhere on campus."

"Sometimes, when he happens to see me," Gail smiled.

"I'll admit you're hard to see," Judy teased.

"I guess if you girls are looking for congeniality, that combination is about as compatible as the United Nations. None of those guys really know each other," Jonie said.

"How about you? Who are you asking?" Trish questioned. Jonie was suddenly center stage, with all eyes on her.

She tossed her socks into the hamper then spoke thoughtfully, "I really don't know."

Judy smiled. "It can't be that difficult."

"That may be easy for you to say. I mean you've been dating pretty regularly. So has Beth. Gail and Linda are on pretty good terms with the guys they're asking, and Trish is practically engaged. Maybe I should stay home and study my speech."

Everyone groaned, then started laughing. "Jonie," Gail scolded, "you know that speech backward and forward."

Judy put her hands up. "Listen a minute. It really is easy to get cold feet about asking a guy for a date unless you are like my roommate, who is never concerned about anything like dates."

"Well, we can't all be as cool as Alyce," Gail interjected.

"Jonie, you must have thought of someone by now," Trish said.

"I did, but, I almost goofed. There is the nicest guy who works in the kitchen but just about the time I got my nerve up, I found out he's going steady."

"How about Tom, Jonie?" Linda asked.

"I'd like to, but I don't know if he'd be interested."

"Come on, Jonie, you must be kidding. Who else around here gets breakfast in bed and the princess treatment the way you do?" Judy wanted to know.

"He's a really nice person, and I don't want to take too much for granted just because he's interested in helping me with my speech."

"Uh huh." Everybody smiled and nodded knowingly. Then Beth said, "And how about the other nine semifinalists? Did they get carnations for breakfast?" This was followed by peals of girlish laughter at Beth's dry humor.

"Another thing, this is Girls' Club invites Boys' Club and Tom lives in the village. He's not Omicron Pi Sigma."

"What about Stan?" Trish asked.

"He's village, also. They both are Aurora Duxes." Jonie's voice was a bit bleak.

"Oh, oh, study period," Beth announced as the bell rang in the halls. She snatched up the towel she was using to dry her long hair and went to the door.

The girls filed out, and Jonie prepared to shower. Gail took her books from the desk and curled up on the bed.

"Jonie," she spoke softly.

"Yes."

"Why don't you ask Chuck?"

Jonie didn't answer.

"You know, every time he goes down the sidewalk out there carrying his books to class, he glances up at this window. I've stood back and watched."

"Maybe he wonders whether you're here," Jonie said, her heart pounding a bit faster.

"Jonie, I know better and so do you. He just doesn't get over you."

"Gail, you still care about Dick, but I notice you aren't going with him."

"And you know," Gail quickly replied, "that it's for an entirely different reason. Dick is not always a Christian. Besides, Dick is quitting school. He leaves Sunday."

"Oh, Gail. I'm so sorry."

"It's his choice. He's changed so much, Jonie. I never told you about last summer when I went to Debby's wedding and spent some time with Dick. He wanted me to do a lot of things I didn't feel right about, and that's when we broke up. He just didn't seem like the same guy I went with in academy. Now he's enlisting in the Air Force. Even Chuck can't talk him out of it."

Jonie turned to her. "Even when it's for the best, it's not easy to stay away from people you really care about. If I went back with Chuck now, it would be the same thing as before. His parents are so concerned about his finishing college and not getting married, et cetera, et cetera. I've got to have some will power and patience and I have to trust that this will all work out right. I've tried to make the best of it and really enjoy college and I can't say I haven't had fun. I think it really is a good idea to get acquainted with all kinds of personalities. When I do get married I will be that much more sure."

"You may be getting acquainted, Jonie, but Chuck is not. He's not even getting good grades, and he was always on the honor roll in academy. He's only dated twice this year, and that was with me, which doesn't count. I know several girls who really like him, but he hardly notices."

"Then he will probably get an invitation to the banquet from someone who will be fun for him to get acquainted with. This will be some lucky girl's chance, anyway."

"I suppose you're right," Gail sighed, concerned for both her friends.

Winter quarter had begun, and a freezing rain had coated the branches with crystal and turned the sidewalks to glass. Jonie made her way gingerly down to the gym to play basketball. She caught up with Jean, her redheaded friend. "Any more garlic parties?" she asked teasingly.

Jean's peals of laughter were infectious. "No, but we are having lots of chives in the sour cream for the baked potatoes at the banquet."

"That's right, you are on the social committee. I'll bet that keeps you busy."

They entered Columbia Auditorium, which served also as the gymnasium. Thirteen girls were gathered to play basketball for the exercise and because they genuinely loved the sport, except when they had to play girls' rules. After a long warmup they organized and played by boys' rules. It was a heated game and kept them running. By the end of the third quarter both teams admitted they were tired, and three of the girls needed to leave, which left a full team on either side, but no substitutes. Della, a stocky sophomore, traveled rapidly up court with the ball and raised her arms to shoot, but the ball never left her hands. Instead she screamed with pain and crumpled to the floor. Jean knelt quickly beside her.

Jonie stood watching in dumb astonishment for a second, then realizing something was seriously wrong, raced to the door calling, "I'll get a doctor." Just as she reached for the knob, it opened for her and, still dashing, she skidded on the ice and sat down neatly between the long legs of a tall, dark-haired fellow.

"You couldn't be in a hurry?" he said, reaching down to give her a hand up.

"Yes, oh, Stan, where's the nearest phone? There's an emergency in there. It's one of the girls."

"Quick, we'll go next door to the bakery. I work there." Holding hands, they ran gingerly on the ice and through the door into the big room fragrant with sweet, familiar odors. Stan grabbed a receiver off the wall phone and asked for the campus clinic. It was only moments before a doctor arrived at the gymnasium.

A group of very serious girls were given a lecture at worship that evening about prolonged strenuous activity and why Della had suffered a heart attack.

Late in the week Jonie finally decided that she would ask Lew. He often dropped by the gym, where she had been spending her spare time. He accepted her invitation. They tossed a few baskets and when she was leaving he offered her a ride to the dorm.

Jonie laughed. "It's only across campus."

"Come," he insisted. "I'll take you to dinner, or are you working tonight?"

"No, I have Thursday nights off."

"Great. My car's here," and he turned toward it at the curb.

Jonie said, "Well, why not? I think the streets are safer than the walks, anyway."

Jonie was a bit surprised when he didn't stop at the cafeteria, and it dawned on her that when Lew said, "I'll take you to dinner" he meant *out* to dinner. In downtown Walla Walla, he pulled into a restaurant.

"Lew, I appreciate this, but I'm certainly not dressed for it."

"You look fine."

"Well, maybe if I leave my coat on," she said, smoothing her hair down with her hands.

Dinner went well, and the ride back to the dorm was filled with soft music and friendly conversation until Lew parked under the trees several blocks from their destination. Within moments, his advances were with intentions that came as a surprise to Jonie.

"Lewis, please," she said firmly, "this is not my idea of a pleasant evening."

For a moment, he was quiet, startled by her rebuff. He was large and muscular and Jonie was no match for him physically. She felt fear rising in her throat, and then he laughed and suddenly there was no mistaking his intentions.

"Oh, God, help me," Jonie breathed. "Lewis, I am going back to the dorm. If you don't care to drive me, I'll walk." He released her, and she got out of the car and walked away in the darkness. Once out of sight, she began to run, her heart pounding. "But, Father, he seemed so nice, so nice! What did I do?"

Jonie was nervous and agitated all through study period. She found it impossible to concentrate, even though Gail was at the library and the room was quiet. She worried over the coming banquet. If he never shows up again, I wouldn't care, she thought. She kept reproaching herself as if she were in some way to blame.

The next day at work in the kitchen one of the upperclassmen who worked there leaned over the deck and whispered to Jonie, "Say, who were you out with last night?"

She looked at him, startled and embarrassed. "How'd you know?"

"Saw you get into his car. I'm surprised at you."

"But I honestly didn't know him or his reputation."

"What about your reputation?" he said, seriously.

"That's what's worrying me, and I had already invited him to the banquet. Now I don't know what to do."

"A nice girl like you needs a big brother like me. After this, ask somebody. I know most of the guys, and that one's not for you, Jonie."

"He seemed nice enough."

"Of course," he shrugged, then looking at her closely, he asked. "Everything OK?"

"Yes, I'm really OK, and please don't tell."

He put his finger over his lips and she flashed a quick smile, thankful for the confidence.

Several times she tried to contact Lewis and found that he had gone for the weekend. Now what to do? "I have no idea whether I should get ready Sunday night or not. Surely, he doesn't expect me to go out with him again." By Saturday afternoon she had a tension headache.

"Father, please help me. I don't want to share this with anyone else, but I need somebody to talk to. Should I just get ready and pretend nothing happened or let myself be sick? I don't want the girls to know. Someone might distort this out of proportion. I have no desire to spend the evening with this character whose company doesn't even appeal to me. Tell me what to do, Father, if he shows up. Amen."

A short time later a beautiful corsage arrived. "OK, Father, I'll go through with it. I'm sure You love him, anyway. I'm glad he's Your child and not mine. I'm sorry, Father, I've got lots to learn myself. Help me to handle this situation as You would have me."

Lew arrived a trifle late, full of apologies for having been detained getting back. Jonie excused him and thanked him for the flowers, which were already in place on the bodice of her dress.

They walked to the auditorium, and Lew talked casually about his trip. They blended into the crowd and ate and drank and enjoyed the entertainment from the stage with the rest of their associates. Jonie relaxed, realizing she had learned a great deal from this experience. I'll be careful where I go and with whom, from now on, she thought. They walked back to the dormitory through the fluffy, falling snowflakes with their friends, and he thanked her for inviting him.

Once Jonie was in her room, she let a long sigh escape her and quickly unpinned the beautiful corsage. Gail looked at her sharply. "You sure haven't been yourself lately."

"I will be now." Jonie smiled in the mirror at her roommate.

There were very few encounters with Lewis after the banquet, but when they chanced to meet on campus he was pleasantly friendly, and Jonie always responded politely. It was a closed chapter in her life and one that taught her the necessary art of saying No.

SUDDEN LOSSES

JONIE WAS most content in art class. There were several artists in her family background, and a love for beauty was instilled early. To have time set aside each week when she could work with pastels or water colors was real enjoyment.

Tom often dropped in to watch her work at some new assignment and very shortly was taking over much of her spare time, also. He encouraged her to join Pegasus, a club that was sponsored by the English department. When she was elected secretary she became involved with the club newsletter. Tom was active in the Sabbath school departments and invited her to teach a primary class of little boys. Jonie's candle was soon burning at both ends, and she sat shivering in her room one evening when Gail and Trish walked in.

"Jonie, why is your face so flushed?" Gail asked.

"Is it?" Jonie reached up, touching her cheek.

Gail came closer. "You have a rash. It's all over your neck, too. Look at you, Jonie. You must have measles or something!"

Trish hurried for the door. "I'll get the dean."

"Oh, Gail, measles are for little kids. I must have had them sometime or other. I can't get sick. My folks will be coming to hear my speech." Jonie was now peering anxiously in the mirror. "I can't be sick," she wailed. "I just can't."

Gail looked distressed. "You'll have to stay in the clinic if you've got something contagious like measles."

"But it can't be that."

"Well, whatever it is, it looks very suspicious."

"I think you are right, Gail," said the dean, coming through the door and taking one look at Jonie. "Come on, young lady, up with the shirt." An alarmed Jonie stared down at some very pink bare skin.

"Looks to me like you have a tummy full." The dean smiled and patted Jonie's shoulder. "You need to be quarantined in the clinic before this spreads all over the dorm. How about you, Gail? Any fever or other symptoms? Put your tongue out."

Gail did so with her face screwed up, wanting to laugh. "I'm not going anywhere. I've had all that kid stuff."

"All right. But you, Jonie, get bundled up good, and I'll drive you to the infirmary and see that you are checked in. I wonder where you contracted this?"

"I think I know. A little boy in my primary Sabbath school class felt bad, and I held him close by my side, then finally took him to his mother. I think I feel about the way he did."

Jonie's problem was diagnosed as scarletina. The nurse helped her take a warm shower, which brought the rash out. She finally fell into a restless sleep and dozed most of the next day also.

She awoke in early evening to find a few amusing messages and cards by her bed, along with a lovely bouquet from Tom. After a light supper the nurse brought in a small radio and plugged it into the wall. "This is by courtesy of a young man who doesn't want you to get behind in current events. Or maybe he wants to be sure you don't forget the sound of his voice."

"Good evening," a deep male voice greeted from the radio, and Jonie smiled. "That's Tom." She listened as he announced the evening news. The nurse smoothed the bed and put the room in order. When the broadcast ended she said, "There was another young man here today asking about you. He seemed very concerned."

"Red hair?" Jonie asked.

"That's right. I see you know him."

"Most of my life, it seems. Wish I could have talked to him," Jonie added, wistfully.

"Well, if you take care now you will be on your feet before you know it." The nurse finished tidying up, put another blanket on the bed, partly opened the window, and turned out the light. Together they had a short prayer, and the nurse left.

In the semidarkness Jonie could see the beautiful bouquet of mixed flowers, but her mind wandered to the meadows of her childhood when she and Chuck were carefree youngsters in grade school. With the window open, the air in her room grew crisp, and she snuggled deeper in the covers. When she was almost asleep a light tapping on the screen brought her wide awake. Reaching over, she pulled the drape aside and saw Chuck's smiling face.

"Why, how did you know I was wishing I could talk to you? I used to always want my mother when I was sick. This time it was you." She laughed softly.

"I never would have guessed," he said. "You'll have me wishing you'd get sick more often. Not really," he added, "because I have been worried about you. I just wanted to find out for myself how you were."

"I'm much better, but how did you know which room I was in?"

He laughed. "It was easy. I bribed the girl who

brought over the dinner trays. She took special notice which room and which window. Pretty risky business," he laughed.

"Won't you get in trouble if you get caught standing there in the bushes?"

"Who's getting caught? The nightwatchman just went by. I made sure of that first."

"I hope he doesn't come back. It's so good to see you."

They had talked quietly through the screen for a few moments when suddenly Chuck dropped out of sight. Jonie held her breath as several faculty members went by on the sidewalk chatting congenially, oblivious to the little drama nearby. After they were safely past, Jonie breathed a long sigh and Chuck popped up again. They laughed nervously, then hurriedly shared a few news items from recent letters they had received from home. They said good night, and Chuck slipped away into the darkness.

This little tête-à-tête broke the barrier that had been growing between them. The tension was gone, and Jonie realized gratefully that whatever happened to them, they would always be friends.

As Jonie rested she said her speech time and time again, preparing for the fateful day just ahead. The rash faded on schedule, and Trish and Judy came to check her out of the clinic and carry her few things back to the dorm. They visited a bit to bring Jonie up to date, then left for their various activities.

Jonie was putting her things away when Gail came in and made a startling announcement, "I may be leaving school."

Jonie turned around in dismay. "Gail, no!"

"I'm afraid so. My mother's not doing too well. I got a letter from Grandma, and it appears I may have to help take care of Mom. We'll see," she said uncertainly.

Jonie sat down thoughtfully. "You know, Gail. I've been so lucky about friends. Each one of them has been so special—you, Linda, and remember Carol, how much she helped me last year at Columbia? How would I have gotten through the year without her? I wish she had taken her nurse's training here instead of California. I thought about all this a few minutes ago when Judy and Trish left the room. Judy is so dear, and I've learned to love Trish. She's always so helpful. She reminded me of Carol today. But it seems that somewhere along the way there's bound to be a parting place for Christian friends. God takes one over here and one over there. That's the way witnessing spreads, I guess. You will always be the most special person I know, and I'll miss you so much if you have to leave, but if God has something for you to do I'll just have to accept that." Jonie glanced up to see tears in Gail's eyes. "Oh, Gail, I'm sorry. I'm thinking about my loss and not about what you must be feeling."

Gail bit her lip, then, after a moment, said, "I'm afraid Mom's drinking problem is about to take her. Even though I hate to leave and I always miss you when we are apart, I've got to do all I can to help Mom, so I know I'll be leaving as soon as Grandma calls."

But in the morning it was Trish who was gone. Her parents had been killed in an auto accident late the night before. Her stunned friends and associates suffered for the sunny-haired girl who had left in the night to care for her younger brother and sisters.

That afternoon Gail received her call and made the necessary arrangements. She left that evening.

Weekend to Remember

TROY PUSHED back the tall white cook's cap and shook his head in puzzlement. The mixture bubbled in the huge kettle, but lacked the thick consistency that would designate it as gravy. "Must need more flour," Troy muttered aloud.

He mixed six more cups of the powdery substance with a little liquid and carefully stirred it into the gravy pot, whistling cheerfully. Soon the lively, bubbling steamed upward again, but the consistency was as thin as before. Troy peered into the kettle, frowning thoughtfully.

Jonie passed with a tray of fruit to set on her end of the deck for supper. She noticed Troy's exasperated expression and called out, "Bad day?"

He was momentarily preoccupied. "No, one of the best days of my life," he answered when her query finally sank in.

"You don't look it."

Troy walked back to the pantry for more flour, whistling again. "After all, it isn't every day one becomes engaged," he told himself. He had found just the person to meet all the qualifications he had long ago mentally listed as being possessed by the ideal minister's wife. Charming, caring, even musical (a real plus).

His mind checked happily down the list as he dipped the quart measure into the bin for another eight cups of flour.

He returned to follow the same procedures as before. But this time his happy preoccupation turned to dismay. It was time to serve, and the gravy still looked like thin, clear broth. Students were even now filing in at the decks.

Jonie walked past Troy and smiled. "I just saw Ellen going by with a bright new Omi pin. "I'll bet you're happy."

"What? Oh, yeah," he grinned. "I hope she knows how to make gravy."

"Why? Having troubles?"

"Sorta." He stuck in a spoon, blew on it and sampled the hot mixture. His eyes widened in disbelief as he grabbed up the kettle and hurriedly dumped the powdered sugar mixture down the sink drain. Jonie giggled as he warned her not to tell. She went back to her place on deck, calling over her shoulder, "Let's hope this is the only time you get engaged."

"You can be sure of that," Troy said with certainty as he buttered and parsleyed the potatoes hoping fervently that no one asked for gravy.

Later, he met Jonie at the time clock. "Tell me how the speech contest is going?" he questioned.

"You're asking me," she said, surprised, "when Ellen is my only female competition?"

"I'd better warn you," said Troy. "She's going to win the finals."

"I wouldn't be surprised," Jonie smiled at his loyalty.

"Yes, she is," Troy stated again.

"You're sure about that?"

"Positive." He was dead serious.

"Wish I had that kind of confidence," Jonie muttered

and hurried away to an appointment with Elder Jenton.

"Good afternoon, Miss Owens. Come into my office, please."

Jonie had not been in Elder Jenton's inner sanctum for several months. She smiled at the now familiar face behind the glasses, wondering what the man had to say to her.

"As you recall, Joan. Jonie, I believe your friends call you."

"Please do the same."

"Thank you. Now, then, I was on the committee that helped select the speakers for tomorrow's chapel period."

"I appreciate the consideration that was given me," Jonie interrupted.

"You deserved it, young lady, and since our last conversation I've done a great deal of thinking about the importance of more youth taking speech classes. I am now in accord with that school of thought. Stick with it, Jonie. You have a very valid point, and I might add, it isn't just the men who have all the talent in those classes. By the way, what do you plan to wear tomorrow?"

"Wear?" Jonie blinked in surprise. "Why, I'm not sure. My black Sabbath dress, maybe."

"Never!" Elder Jenton frowned behind the glasses. "Forgive me if I am speaking out of turn, but if you don't mind an old man's suggestion, what you wore the other night would be just right."

"The red top with the white wool skirt?"

"Yes, yes, that's the one."

Jonie smiled and shrugged. "That advice I will take, and thank you."

Jonie woke up the second morning after Gail's

departure feeling the loss keenly, and then she remembered that her folks would be arriving sometime before chapel. She sprang out of bed before the alarm went off and put her room in order before going to work. Snow had fallen all night long and continued through the morning. Jonie checked between classes, but her family had not arrived or called by chapel time. She felt a little concerned as she stood backstage in Columbia Auditorium.

"Father," she prayed, "I need Your help so much today and please protect my folks wherever they are. Help my speech to go well and help the other four who are taking part also. Thank You."

She looked up to see Troy on the back steps, his hand clasping Ellen's, their heads bowed silently. Jonie smiled, "With support like that how can she lose?"

When the participants took their places on the platform Jonie looked searchingly through the packed building. There was no sign of her parents, and she couldn't help feeling very disappointed.

Jonie was seated in the middle of the stage behind the large podium. She listened intently to the first two speeches, and then it was her turn. She walked forward and took her place, pausing for a moment. Then she saw a familiar black hat bobbing about directly in front of her on the third row. A broad smile lighted Jonie's face as she looked into the eyes of her proud parents. With new verve she gave her salutation to the mayor, her professors, her friends, and, last but not least, to her parents, who had come such a long way through the storm. Then she began her speech.

"Oh, no!" the words echoed vibrantly through the auditorium, "the alcohol problem does not affect *us*. Why, *we* are a group of people who do not drink. But let me tell you, we cannot say, 'Why worry about it, we are not affected,' for alcohol has just hit a homer on this campus.

"Three days ago in my dormitory, beautiful Trish with her golden hair and happy ways departed suddenly in the night. There was never a problem of drinking in their home but *someone, somewhere* had that problem. Trish's parents were driving sanely and safely, but were met on a curve by a speeding, intoxicated driver who couldn't see the middle line.

"Trish, a younger brother, and two small sisters are now orphans. It took a matter of moments and some booze to wipe out some pretty fine parents. Aren't you glad they were not yours?

"That same day Walla Walla College lost another promising student who went home to care for an alcoholic mother, dying from cirrhosis of the liver. I have loved and laughed, studied and worked my way through school with Gail during four years in academy and this year at college. Her sunny disposition often knew the grief that came tumbling from the contents of one bottle after another.

"And we sit complacently ignoring the death toll mounting each year from liquor! Think about it. Even though you may not drink, let me ask each of you, how often has alcohol hit a homer in your life or at least made it to second or third base?"

Tom shifted in his seat to get a better look at the stage from his position in the back. Elder Jenton leaned forward in the balcony. Both were thinking, "Forceful, dynamic, but what happened?" This wasn't Jonie's original speech. From somewhere deep within her, anger was rising, an anger that was tearing at her as the very personal memories of an alcohol-broken home years ago rose to the surface.

She was gripping the podium, leaning forward

toward the microphone and spontaneously reacting to the rapt attention before her. In a few moments she easily made the transition back into her original speech. She finished with a plea to the youth in the audience to become involved even if it was in a small way, such as pushing subscriptions for *Listen* magazine.

"Or shall we sit idly in our apathy until we are hit by one of alcohol's many, tragic homers?"

There was complete silence throughout the building as she sat down. There had been a tiger in Jonie during those few moments. The audience had caught her spirit, and the usual polite clapping became a pandemonium of cheers and stomping.

Jonie was astonished. Her mother was swallowing tears. Tom hurried outside and around the building to the back door to wait for the triumphant orator. "I can't believe it!" he kept saying to himself, as the applause escaped through the windows.

In another few minutes the speeches were finished, and Jonie hurried to her parents. Tom followed her through the crowd. "You were sensational, really you were, Jonie. And the applause, wasn't that something? It would have broken an applause meter. I couldn't believe the judges chose Ellen!"

"I'm so glad they did." Jonie smiled delightedly. "She's such a dear, and Troy is one of the finest men I know. The prize money will go toward a very special event, I'm sure."

Jonie hardly heard Tom's answer as she rushed into her parents' arms. "You made it! I was so worried!" she cried.

"I was afraid you would be," her mother said. "We had car trouble in The Dalles."

"We left the car in a garage and took the train," her father added. "Your mother was so afraid we'd miss your speech. We just *had* to be here."

"We barely got in the door. There was no way to let you know we had arrived, so we asked someone whether they could find us seats down front so you'd know, and it worked out fine. We are so proud of you."

Tom stood close by, smiling at the family scene before him. Jonie suddenly noticed. "Oh, I forgot! I'm sorry. This is Tom Harrison. I told you about him at Christmas time. He's the one who coached me."

"Well, you did a fine job," her father said, pumping Tom's hand.

"Thank you, sir. I don't deserve any credit, though. May I invite you all to dinner, or do you have other plans, Jonie?"

"I've made arrangements here, but you're welcome to eat with us." They made their way out of the crowd into the drifting flakes.

A tall young man with dark curly hair stopped Jonie to congratulate her, as did several others. Mrs. Owens was enjoying it more than her daughter.

Later the two women went to the dormitory. In the room, Jonie confided that even though she missed Gail, it was nice to have her mother alone and all to herself.

Donna Owens agreed. "Now tell me about Tom. He seems to like you a lot."

"We are just good friends. We have fun together. He's going to take me to a radio station next week to watch him broadcast."

"That should be interesting. And who was the boy who stopped you on the sidewalk—the one with romance written all over his face?"

"Oh, Mother! You romanticist. That was Stan. He's a premed student whom I really like a lot, but unfortunately he seldom dates. I'd like to get better acquainted. We do ski together now and then, but premeds hit the books hard and avoid serious relationships as a rule."

"Sounds like wisdom," her mother nodded. "Now what's your next big project? You always seem to have one."

"I hope to write a radio script in spring quarter. I've always wanted to, and Tom has gotten me all the more interested."

"You probably will, then," her mother said, laughing at her daughter's enthusiasm.

While her father visited a schoolmate from his own years at Walla Walla College, Jonie and her mother shared the kind of secrets a girl tells only her closest friend.

Saturday night Tom took them all out to dinner and then to the depot. The two young people followed the Owenses onto the train to visit for a last few minutes while waiting for it to pull out. All too soon, the train was rolling down the track and picking up momentum. Tom and Jonie, still aboard, stared at each other in consternation.

"Conductor, Conductor, sir." Tom called out to the man entering the car from the other end. "Is there any way you can get us off?"

"Off? Off, you say?"

"That's right!"

The conductor ran back out of the car. He returned momentarily with a lantern and leaned precariously out the door swinging the light in an arc. The engine was going around a curve, and when the engineer saw the signal the train gradually slowed. "You'll have to jump," the conductor shouted at Tom.

"Jonie, be careful," her mother said, coming up beside her.

"Tom, you'll catch her?" Mr. Owens looked concerned.

"Yes, sir." Tom leaped into a snowbank, ran beside the train a few steps and reached out to Jonie, who jumped very neatly into his arms. Her parents looked relieved as they caught their last glimpse of Tom and Jonie laughing together in the snow as the train rumbled on down the track.

The two young people waved from their soft snowdrift to the curious travelers in the cars that rolled past them. They were still laughing at the trip they had almost taken.

"Tom," Jonie shouted above the noisy *clackety-clack* on the track, "you have just shared one of the most memorable weekends of my life. Thanks for everything."

He turned and looked at her. The wind was playing in her long dark hair and lifting the end of her winter scarf. She was covered with snow, and her nose was red. He leaned over and kissed her lightly on the cold tip end of it. She smiled shyly, and he kissed her once more with tenderness.

The Proposal

JONIE AND Linda stood the two bikes in the rack. Tom checked the tires on his and put it away also.

"Thank you, Tom, for renting these. I've enjoyed the afternoon so much," Jonie said.

"And I appreciated being included," Linda added.

"My pleasure, girls. It just seemed like a great way to greet spring."

"Drinking in this kind of fresh air is almost intoxicating," Linda remarked.

"Addictive," Jonie corrected.

"I'll agree with that." Tom smiled.

They strolled back to the campus, and Linda stopped at the music building to practice. Tom and Jonie went on toward the speech department. When they walked in Tom picked up a pile of mail to sort. Most of it was advertising. He suddenly looked at Jonie with a peculiar expression. "Jonie, remember that contest you entered with your radio script?"

"You mean they wrote back?"

"Looks like it's from Radio City, New York," he said, holding up an envelope.

Jonie ripped it open and gasped as she read the exciting message.

"Tom, they've accepted my script. I didn't win one of

the prizes, but, look, they sent me a check. I can't believe
it."

"I can." He laughed with delight.

"They actually accepted it," Jonie shook her head in
amazement, "but Miss Hammond despairs over my
writing. I may even flunk freshman comp."

"I doubt that that ever keeps you from being in print,
Jonie." Tom watched her as she stared in disbelief at the
check then read the letter once again.

She sat down on the desktop beside him and sighed
with happiness. "You've been a great friend, Tom."

"I hope so." He laid down the mail and turned toward
her.

"You have helped me with so many things," she
added.

"I've considered that a special privilege," he
answered. "You are a real pleasure to be with, Jonie,
and there is something I want to talk to you about.
Earlier this week I was over at the men's hall and
listened to several guys discussing their women and
how they felt girls preferred honesty—you know,
putting everything on the level so the girl is not
constantly guessing about things."

"Of course!" Jonie answered.

"I'm in love with you, Jonie. I want you to marry me."

She eyed him solemnly, but did not respond.

Tom slipped off the desk and stood in front of her. "I
know you want to finish your education, and I would
want you to. I have a call to teach at La Sierra College,
and if we got married right after my graduation this
spring we could move down to California. I would teach,
and you could get your degree."

Jonie studied his face in astonishment.

"Leave here?" she said, almost boring a hole through
the tabletop with her index finger.

"I know you love Walla Walla College and we could even stay here if you preferred. I could keep my job at the radio station and put you through school."

"Tom, you are very generous, but you hardly know me."

"What do you mean, I hardly know you? Whose acquaintance do you think I've been cultivating these past few months?"

"I mean, there is so much you don't know about me."

"What are you referring to?"

"Well, you don't know if I can cook, what kind of housekeeper I'd be, or even whether I like children. We've never discussed those things."

"Now, listen, it's obvious you like children. Half your Sabbath school class follows you around campus. I'm sure you're a very neat housekeeper. [That made her smile.] You are, aren't you?"

"Much better since I don't have a roommate to pick up after me," Jonie said, laughing.

He looked almost stern in his seriousness, and she sobered instantly.

"And, as far as cooking goes," he continued, "I like all my vegetables creamed."

"Yuk!" she exclaimed. "I hate creamed vegetables!"

He looked distressed. "Jonie, I'm very serious. I love you, and I'm sure these minor problems can be worked out."

She sat quietly looking at him for a long moment without speaking.

"Jonie, do you love me at all?"

"I do care very much about you, Tom."

"But you don't love me."

"I don't know. I've honestly not thought about it."

"Is it someone else?"

"Oh, Tom, please don't press me."

"Of course not. Just don't say No. Think about it, please. Take all the time you need."

She slipped down from the desk. "I'm sure you've prayed about it. Now it's my turn. I don't want to hurt anyone. You are so very special. Please give me time to know what's right and don't call me for a few days. I need to think and pray."

A disturbed Jonie left the office and walked back to the empty room. A new roommate was coming Monday for spring quarter, but for the present, she could talk to the Lord and be alone. She knelt by the window facing the campus with its parade of red and yellow tulips and lacy mountain ash. Instinctively, her eyes lifted to the sky. "Father, I need to care more, if this is what You want me to do. I know Tom would see to it that our first priority would be finishing school. That's very attractive. It's been such a struggle all year trying to work and keep up with the tuition, and it would be so much easier on my parents if I got married. But, Father, what about Tom? It would be so unfair to him unless I really love him as a wife should love her husband. Oh, Father, would I? I just don't know, I just don't know. I suppose that would come, but why did this all happen now? I just don't feel ready for such a commitment, or is it the feelings I still have for Chuck? Father, why must I feel so confused? I love You, Father. Please help me to keep that love foremost in my life."

Jonie tucked her anxieties away, but kept to herself the entire weekend, often seeking Heaven within her heart.

Enrika moved in on Monday, bringing with her a whole new atmosphere. She was as bright and colorful as a prism in the sun. She was about the same size as Gail and less serious, though she was a good student and intent on becoming a nurse. She always saw the funny side of everything and had the delightful ability to laugh more easily at herself than at others. Jonie loved her instantly and felt fortunate to have her for a roommate.

With all nature bursting with new energy, the tennis courts became a favorite spot. Riki and Jonie were in the spring class of beginners. "I'll never get the hang of scoring," Jonie complained, after the first lesson.

Riki's black eyes danced. "As long as you score with love?"

Jonie sighed. "I think I'd rather not." She had avoided Tom for several days, and he had left her alone as agreed. Returning to the room Tuesday afternoon, she found a bouquet of beautiful daffodils and carnations on the dresser, along with a box of expensive chocolates. They had been sent by Tom.

Riki exclaimed. "Jonie, you haven't told me about this!"

"I really don't know what to tell you—yet."

Eight-year-old Mickey was riding his scooter down the sidewalk in front of the dormitory when a bolt fell out of the wheel. A tall, red-haired young man carrying a small package was coming down the walk. He knelt to help the boy with his problem. He laid the package on the step, picked up the bolt and nut close at hand, and with experienced fingers soon put the wheel on the scooter and a smile on Mickey's face.

"Boy, you're a whiz! Thanks a lot!" The freckles moved into the pleasant creases that accompanied a wide, grateful grin.

"You're welcome."

"Hey, what's in the package?" the child asked curiously.

"This happens to be Almond Roca for someone pretty special."

"Oh, a girl?"

"That's right."

"What's her name?"

"Jonie."

"Jonie Owens?"

"Yes, do you know her?"

"Yep. She's my Sabbath school teacher and she just got a huge box of candy from our leader. He brought her a bunch of flowers, too. Boy, she must like candy a lot. So do I." This last hopefully.

The young man turned to go up the steps, then stood for a long moment before entering. When Jonie was summoned to the parlor she was surprised to find that her caller was Chuck.

"I came to tell you goodbye, Jonie."

"Goodbye?" She was stunned.

"Yes, I decided not to continue spring quarter."

"You're quitting! But why?"

"There just isn't much sense in sticking around. Here, I brought you this small box of your favorite candy just to say goodbye."

"Thank you. You know how I like Almond Roca, but I don't understand why you are quitting."

"Once I went to Columbia Academy because you were there," he said. "I came here wanting to be near you. Now I hear you are marrying Tom. Do you think I care to stick around? It would be almost a sin to be on the same campus and see you every day going to classes and know you were married to someone else when I feel as I do about you."

"Oh, Chuck, I've not said I'll marry Tom."

"But you are planning on it, and I don't want to be here, so I'm leaving in the morning."

Jonie felt a strange emotion surging into her throat. "Now, you listen a minute, Chuck. I have not promised to marry anyone and I'm not planning to marry anyone until the Lord lets me know who and when. Go home if you want, but don't blame such a foolish mistake on me. Remember that old cliché, 'Faint heart never won fair lady'? Well, fair ladies never consider quitters!" She whirled around, leaving a stunned young man watching her ascend the stairs.

During study period Jonie stayed in her room alone to finish a written assignment and then she retired early. She fell asleep easily in the warm darkness to be awakened by a light tap and the monitor's stepping in. The girl said softly, "Jonie, I hate to wake you, but the dean wants you to come to her office."

Jonie slipped quickly out of bed and into her robe, wondering what the dean could want of her, or had she made some mistake for which she was being called on the carpet for reprimand? In the dean's office, she was relieved to be greeted by a cheerful smile.

"Sit down, Jonie. I'm sorry if you were already in bed, but I have not had much time to talk with you since last quarter when you were ill and fainted during your speech. How have you been? Everything all right?"

"Must be. I don't dare gain another pound and I've never felt better."

"Well, you do look vibrant. Your social life must be satisfactory?" Jonie nodded. "I have a special reason for asking," the dean continued.

"Oh," Jonie was instantly alert.

"You know, it's very satisfying to see our young men choose Christian girls to share their future with. And if they graduate before that choice is made, I'll admit it is a concern."

Jonie's eyes widened, then narrowed as she became

aware of what the dean was referring to. But how could she know, the girl wondered.

"You see, Joan, sometimes we see our young people graduate and leave here to take positions for which they have prepared themselves, yet they have neglected some aspect of their lives, maybe the spiritual or perhaps the social part. It is disheartening to feel we have some way failed in assisting them in becoming well-rounded whole individuals."

"I think I understand what you are trying to tell me, Mrs. Spring."

"I'm sure you do. That's why I am so pleased that one of our most promising seniors has found someone who is a Christian before he leaves this place. My dear, he is such a fine choice."

Jonie began to fidget uncomfortably. Could it be that she was being given an answer to her many prayers through this advice? Suddenly she became very calm and her hands lay quietly in her lap.

"Mrs. Spring, what you say makes a great deal of sense, and I think it's beautiful that on this campus the faculty care enough to worry about their seniors leaving without a Christian mate, or at least a promised one. I realize that Satan is always looking for opportunities to assist in the unequally yoked type of marriage, and it must be much easier to make those kinds of matches away from friends of one's own faith."

"That's right, dear. Then you do understand what I'm trying to say." The woman smiled.

"Absolutely!" Jonie answered. "However, I don't believe that a difference in religious convictions is the only way of being unequally yoked, nor do I feel that it would be necessary to commit myself to some promising young graduate just to guarantee his union with a Christian mate before leaving this campus.

"I appreciate what you are saying, but somehow it seems to me that I will know without a doubt what God would choose for me. I have just realized that I do not have those answers. I'm sorry if that disappoints anyone, but I can only depend on God's judgment in this matter. It is just too important, and I would be doing Tom a great injustice if I were to encourage this any further, feeling as uncertain as I do."

A smile broke the serious expression on the dean's face. "Jonie, I'll have to admit I am relieved. Now I have a confession. Tom was here today with a gift for you and he visited some little time with me. He very much cares for you and requested that I perhaps influence you in his favor. I can see you have the situation well in hand, and with God's help you will make the right decision."

"That's the only way I can be confident," Jonie answered. "A lifetime is a long time to be sorry."

The dean nodded in agreement.

The following day Tom stopped by the art department where Jonie was working on a winter scene much like some of the places they had hiked together. The icy stream, the leaning alder, and stately pines were just losing their cloak of winter snow in an early spring thaw with Jonie's last few strokes.

"How beautiful!" Tom said, coming up softly behind her. "An exquisite piece of art done by my favorite artist."

Jonie took the picture from the easel. "Then you shall have it," she said, putting it into his hands.

"I am delighted," he said, with pleasure. "I'll find the frame this deserves. Many, many thanks."

Jonie had remained after class to finish her painting, and the room was empty. "This time the pleasure and the privilege are mine. I can't think of anyone who has ever treated me nicer or been more interested in

encouraging the development of any small talent I
might have."

"Jonie, Jonie, you don't owe me anything."

"Tom, I made this for you with love. I mean that
sincerely, and my response to the greatest compliment
you have ever given me is with love, also. I cannot marry
you."

Stunned disbelief slowly erased the pleasure on
Tom's face.

"Is that final?" he asked quietly.

"Yes, Tom. I have no doubt that God has someone
else who will make you much happier than I could.
Please believe that."

He continued to look at her for a long moment. Then
he turned toward the door, carrying the woodland scene.

"Tom," Jonie called after him, "please pray for both
of us." He paused and nodded but did not look back.

Another easel stood nearby and on it stood the
unfinished portrait of a child. Jonie turned to finish the
assignment, and for some reason she gave the hair
coppery highlights.

Spiritual Emphasis Week

RIKI KICKED the door gently, shut it with her foot, and dumped her books on the bed. "Whew, those steps will do me in. I hear they are going to tear this building down and add on to Conard."

"If they move us across campus, that means no more watching the matches on the tennis courts below our window." Jonie was intent on the game below.

Riki joined her. "Our room is a great location for a bird's-eye view. Jonie, who's that fellow in the second court?"

Jonie's eyes traveled the courts. "The one with the crippled right arm? That's Ted."

"He's really good."

"I know, and not just at tennis, but every sport, even football. And watching him ice skate is something else. The way he compensates for his balance is beautiful. He skates like a pro."

"Why does he keep his thumb through his belt loop? What happened anyway?"

"I suppose since he doesn't have any use or control of his arm, owing to polio he had as a child, he tucks it out of the way more or less."

"It sure doesn't slow him down. Look at that slam! He's all over the court."

"Gail went out with him a few times. Wendy has dated him a lot. He's very funny, has a marvelous wit. He's not a church member, though."

"How did he happen to come to Walla Walla College?"

"That's Russ he's playing. He invited him to attend. Ted has lived a pretty rough life, but had such a high regard for Russ he somehow decided to give this a try."

"I wonder what he thinks now. I mean, Week of Prayer, and all."

"Hard to say, I'm sure. It's a big change from the streets of San Francisco."

During Spiritual Emphasis Week a tall, dark-haired young evangelist with a winning smile and a convincing message assisted by the Holy Spirit touched many hearts, though, of course, there were some unmoved and disinterested students. During the week small groups met each evening in prayer bands to petition the Lord for the things closest to their hearts. Jonie's group decided to pray particularly for Ted, one of the most colorful young men on campus, who had not yet become acquainted with the extraordinary power of prayer. Several times a day, separately and collectively, the girls prayed for Ted.

It was Friday evening when Pastor Vandeman made a special appeal to anyone who felt the Saviour's gentle calling. From the side balcony Jonie pleaded with her heavenly Father for that very special person whom she hardly knew. The aisles below filled with students quietly making their way to the front in answer to the call to give their young lives to the Master. Beneath the facing balcony across from her, two young men rose with tears streaming down their cheeks, and each with an arm about the other's shoulder, made their way to the front together. Tears blurred Jonie's eyes as she saw

Russ supporting his friend Ted in the greatest of all decisions. "Oh, Father, thank You. You heard and You answered."

Jonie would have been even more grateful for the decision made that night could she have known the future, for the following year her dear friend Gail became Ted's wife.

During the final meeting on Sabbath morning Jonie prayed earnestly for herself. She prayed, not only for a forgiveness of her mistakes and a closer walk with her Master but also that she would somehow know what she should do with her life. At that moment, she had no other desire but that she receive guidance about the right career.

Jonie was sitting on the front row of the main floor, and just above her on the rostrum the evangelist was praying reverently that each would wait on the Lord to give them the answers in those very important issues of the future, be it a career, a mate, or the decision to follow the Lord. Following that prayer, Jonie opened her eyes to take her seat. Her fleeting glance crossed the auditorium and, to her surprise, met the very serious eyes of Chuck. "Father, is this my answer?" she breathed. Suddenly, there was a settled feeling of peace and happy contentment within her.

The week of serious commitments was followed by a Saturday night of volleyball and relay races in the gym. Most of the girls in Jonie's hall attended with dates. Jonie went alone, with no regrets. She had to admit that the evening of freedom and feeling available again was fun. She was gently teased by Linda and Judy, but wasn't the least concerned.

"Why on earth sit in the room and miss all the fun just because nobody asks you? It certainly doesn't take men to make the world go around. Besides, how else do I let them know I'm available," she quipped.

There were peals of laughter at that contradiction. The evening was fun, and the activity pleasantly tiring. When it was over, Jonie tumbled into bed, and with the pleasant awareness that she had Sunday morning off, slept hard and long. Riki was gone when she awoke.

Jonie sat up suddenly and looked out the window. "Of all the strange dreams," she muttered. Suddenly she missed Chuck terribly. She dressed quickly and went to the telephone. "Oh, I know he will be working," she told herself a bit anxiously as she dialed.

But in a moment she heard the familiar voice on the wire. "Oh, Chuck, I'm so glad you're there. Have you any mail from home? I've heard no news for so long. I think I'm homesick."

"Sure, I've got a letter that came yesterday from Mom. I'll be right over."

Jonie hung up and waited impatiently. Her dark hair was tumbled, she was in Sunday jeans, old tennis shoes, and a sloppy sweater, but the smile was all Chuck saw when he came through the door of the front lobby.

"The letter!" he said, grinning and holding it just out of her reach.

"Are you going to torment me?" she pouted, straining to reach it.

"Now, let me see. What will you trade for this valuable and important missive?"

"I could tell you what I dreamed last night, but you wouldn't believe me."

"All right, I guess I can settle for that. Try me," he ordered.

"Well, I dreamed we were in a blue car and we'd driven quite a ways. We were on the Oregon coast and we stopped in front of a row of cottages."

The raised arm holding the letter dropped slowly as a

peculiar expression crossed Chuck's face as she spoke. He continued, "And the cottages were gray with pink flower boxes and the wooden lawn chairs . . ."

It was Jonie's turn to be startled. ". . . were also painted pink," she finished his sentence, then asked, "Chuck, how could you have known I dreamed last night that we were honeymooning?"

"Jonie, would you believe, I dreamed the exact, the very exact same thing, even to the pink furniture on the lawn?" They leaned against the wall in the open hallway staring at each other in disbelief.

She broke the silence with a whisper, "Chuck, please marry me someday."

His eyes searched hers before answering. "Are you sure?" he questioned softly.

She nodded, her eyes never leaving his. "Positive," she answered.

Suddenly, he was holding her, and when the dean opened her office door at that moment, she quickly shut it again, smiling to herself at the kiss she had just witnessed.

A few moments later a blood-curdling yahoo, louder than that of a Comanche Indian, echoed down the sidewalk and a tall redhead was seen running toward Sittner Hall.

Someone From the Past

"WHAT I want to know, Jonie, is how do you gracefully say, 'Sorry, sir, I'm just not interested. You see, I'm engaged now.'"

"Riki, stop it!" Jonie couldn't help laughing at her roommate's tone of mock sophistication. "News circulates. Besides, it's not as though I had any great following."

"Well, Stan was here asking for you while I worked at the front desk today. I'm sure it was for Saturday night."

"Stan!"

"Yes, and I quickly said, 'Wasn't that something—about Jonie's getting engaged Sunday?' He looked surprised, then excused himself and left. I know he felt embarrassed."

"But I gave up on Stan months ago. I really didn't think he was very interested. I'm sorry if he was embarrassed. I really liked him."

"And what about Tom, Jonie?"

"Riki," Jonie's tone betrayed her irritation, "what does a girl do—get a soapbox and announce that she's out of circulation? A guy in Pegasus asked me for a date for a club party at one of the faculty homes for this Saturday night. I'll admit it was a little awkward."

"What did you tell him?" Riki asked.

"I said, 'Why, I'm flattered, but I'm afraid it might only lead to bloodshed since I just got engaged.' He just laughed and agreed. Chuck is bringing his club pin over before supper tonight. Then I can join the ranks of the unavailable females on this campus, and nobody need be embarrassed."

Riki nodded. "Too bad we can't stamp the taken males with something visible, not that those minute pins are the most obvious."

"You're right about that," Jonie agreed, as she headed out the door to meet Chuck on her way to work.

From a large tray Jonie lined the deck with tall parfait glasses of prune whip. Each was capped with cream topping and a cherry. *I'm not exactly fond of prune whip, but they do look pretty,* she thought.

Troy stood over her with another tray balanced carefully on one steady, practiced hand. Suddenly he shouted, "Jonie's got an Omi pin!" Abruptly, without warning, as he stood smiling at Jonie's blushing face while all attention focused on her, the heavy tray teetered clumsily. The parfait glasses slid off balance and came down in a jumble. Jonie's head was crowned with purple goop, trimmed with white fluff and red cherries. The crash and tinkle of broken glass held the attention of both lines of students going through deck with their supper trays. Everyone was laughing uproariously as Troy used his apron to mop up the mortified Jonie, who stared at the embarrassed boy with both disgust and amusement through the purple mask.

"I guess that's one way to announce my engagement!" she sputtered. "I know you are an aspiring theologian, but you needn't be in such a rush to perform baptisms." She checked out and headed for the showers as the news of her engagement spread through the dining room.

In the dormitory she was teased, but confided to Riki that she was thankful only the boys were ducked in the fish pond when they got engaged, not that she hadn't needed it after Troy's announcement.

Jonie's pleasure heightened when Chuck's folks gave their blessing and encouraged a summer wedding. "We know you love each other, and even though we feel that you're too young for this step, we will join you in an effort to pull it all together and see you back into school next fall."

After their weekend visit, Jonie had difficulty studying. Spring fever was afflicting the entire campus, and with only a few weeks left in the term, it was hard to concentrate. Monday afternoon she was sitting at the desk in front of the window with her mail, looking at an envelope addressed to her in an unfamiliar hand. The name in the upper left corner sent a strange quiver through her, and she could not bring herself to open it. For many moments it lay on the desk, and Jonie stared at it as though seeing into the past. She could hear her mother's voice echoing in her mind. "You are becoming a woman, Jonie, and someday your real father will show up and expect to take his beautiful young daughter out on his arm and show her off."

"Oh, Mother, how could such a thing ever happen?"

"You'll see. It will happen. It sometimes worries me."

"But we haven't seen him in years. The divorce was when I was so young, before we were even Christians. I am Jonie Owens now. I appreciate my Christian home and all that you and Dad have tried to do for me. I could never be interested in my biological father's life style."

"I hope not, dear," her mother answered.

"And, besides," Jonie continued, "when you were all

alone struggling to make a living for us, and Dad came along, he introduced you to this wonderful belief and opened the door to Christian education for me. Do you think I can ever forget that or appreciate him enough?"

Jonie had been very adamant in her statement that day. Now, with the letter unopened, she felt unsure. If I open this, will my world change? she asked herself.

She was always one to rip open letters impatiently, but now she reached into the desk drawer and drew out the silver letter opener. Slowly and carefully, she slipped the slim blade under the flap and unsealed it meticulously.

"My Darling Daughter," she read, "for years you have been in my thoughts. I carried your picture with me through the war. Many times I took it out and studied it when the going was rough. I would try to imagine how the little girl I once held in my arms could be changing, growing up into a young woman.

"I spent time in Germany after the war was ended and participated in the mop-up operations. I have now returned to the States and with great difficulty I have been able to locate you again. My greatest desire is to see you. Of course, I will leave that entirely up to you, but I do hope you will grant me that pleasure.

"Please write or call me collect.

"Your loving father."

Jonie laid the letter aside and stared out the window at the bright clouds being carried on the spring breeze. Again, she heard her mother's voice. "Someday your real father will show up. Someday your real father——" Torn by her mother's concern and her loyalties to her stepfather, whom she had long considered the completion of their family unit, Jonie slipped to her knees almost automatically. "Oh, heavenly Father, what do I do about this? What do I do?" She dropped her head on the desk and waited. Unbelievably soon the answer crossed her mind, *Go and see Professor Jenton.* Of course! After all, he is my adviser, she thought. I'll pray that he will be objective and help me make the right decision. She hurried to his office with the letter, hoping he would be there and would have time for her.

Elder Jenton smiled and motioned Jonie in when he saw her standing in the doorway. "How is the great orator today?" he asked, teasingly.

"Perplexed," she answered.

"Anything I can help you with?"

"I'm hoping so."

"Well, sit down and tell me all about it."

She handed him the letter. He read it, then sat thoughtfully quiet for a moment. Presently, he spoke.

"Your name is not Owens?"

"Not legally. I took it with my mother's marriage. I consider myself Jonie Owens."

"Are you close to your stepfather?"

She nodded. "He has always been very good to me. It was because of him and his mother that we joined this church."

"How did that happen?"

"You mean you want to hear the whole story?"

"Yes, if you care to tell me."

"As a girl, my mother was in a boarding school for young women preparing to be nuns. Being musically talented and very spiritual, she had two ambitions—to play the large pipe organ in the cathedral and to become a nun like Sister Teressa, who knelt on the sunroom balcony in the early dawn each day to pray. Mother received instruction on the organ and realized her first ambition, but not the second, because she met my father while visiting home. They fell in love, and that was the end of her ambitions to become a nun."

Elder Jenton smiled, and Jonie continued. "My mother was a beautiful girl from a very comfortable home in an elite neighborhood. My father was from a large family of rather poor circumstances. They were much too young when they married and from vastly different backgrounds. With the great depression making life difficult and my father's taste for drinking developing, the marriage was doomed almost from the start.

"After the separation my mother tried to make a living scrubbing floors in an ice-cream parlor. She worked all night, but we always went to the nearest church on Sunday morning. It was in a Christian church that mother met Jesus and became deeply committed. This was during a period of great trial and unhappiness in her life.

"One night she had a peculiar dream. She saw a scroll unrolling. One by one, she read each of the first three commandments written on it but the fourth was missing. Instead, she saw a beautiful scene of heaven, the river and the tree of life. Then the rest of the commandments on the scroll continued through the tenth. She then saw Jesus standing in her room holding out His nail-scarred hand to her. But, try as she would, her head would not lift to see His radiant countenance. She awoke sitting up in bed in a cold sweat. 'Oh, no!' she exclaimed, 'I've been breaking the fourth commandment. I mopped the floor last Sunday.'"

"Not long after that she met my stepfather and his mother, from whom she received Bible studies, learned about the Sabbath, and was later baptized. So, you see, I feel a great deal of appreciation to him for giving me the opportunities I've had, to know my Saviour better. I also feel a deep sense of loyalty to my family. I would hate to hurt my mother by seeing this man whom I really don't even know. I just don't know what to do."

Elder Jenton snapped forward in his chair, peering over his glasses at her and holding up the letter. "But, Jonie, this man *is* your father. He also has a right to salvation, and it may be he will find it through his association with his Christian daughter. By no means should you neglect this opportunity. Keep that in mind as you pray for guidance in this matter."

It was a very solemn girl who left the office of her adviser after his counsel and prayer with her. She felt she had received her answer. One evening a few days later she descended the stairway feeling more nervous and apprehensive than with any new date she could remember. Waiting for her at the bottom of the stairs was the stranger who was her father.

A tall handsome man with shiny black hair, he smiled as she approached, and a flood of near-forgotten memories washed over her. She was a very little girl again, begging him for a bedtime story, and being charmed by his talking fiddle. Standing in the middle of her bedroom, his black shoes as shiny as his hair, he made the violin talk up and down the strings for her amusement. Then he played a lullaby, and she fell asleep.

Now, at this moment, he was holding out his hand to her as he said softly, "I would have known you anywhere. You are so very like your mother."

The evening passed swiftly as father and daughter became acquainted over dinner at an elegant restaurant. Soft music played in the background, and a few couples circled the floor. Watching her quizically, he invited her to dance. When she declined he seemed disappointed, then suggested ordering cocktails. When she shook her head he suddenly realized that Jonie's way of life was completely different from his own.

As they waited for dinner, he took a small package from his pocket. "Before I left Europe, I was in charge of a group of young Germans who were assisting in the cleanup operations after the war. I felt sorry for some of them. It seemed to me that those boys could eat a bit more if they had it, so I'd scrounge our mess hall after breakfast for all the leftover hot cakes, portions of jam, and whatever remained in the bottoms of the cans that just got thrown out anyway. I took this food to these German boys, and they seemed appreciative and became friendly.

"There was one very young fellow who saw me take your picture from my billfold, and he asked about it. I told him it was your birthday and I hoped to see you someday. He took this little box from his pocket and said, 'I would be so honored to know this was hers.' I notice that you do not wear jewelry, Jonie, but this beautiful little ring is a keepsake I want you to have."

Jonie opened the box and studied the gold circle with its dainty jewels winking in the candlelight. "To think this beautiful little gift, with all its memories of sadness brought on by a war now resolved in a friendship stretching across continents, is actually mine." She smiled up at him. "I will treasure it."

He watched her fondly. "You know I'm very proud of you even with all your peculiar ideas. Your mother did a good job rearing you. Tell me, what are your future plans?"

"I will be getting married this summer," she told him.

"You don't say!" he said with interest. "And what is your young man like?"

"The finest."

He laughed. "I'm sure he is if you think so."

"He really is. I've known that since we were children

together in grade school. He's the greatest."

"Well, I guess you *should* know then."

"It's strange how there was always this big question about anyone I dated. 'What is he *really* like without his best foot forward to impress me?' With Chuck, it's different. He never tries to impress anyone. He is always just himself. I know him in all his moods—angry, irritated, or short-tempered, but always kind. He is fun-loving, humorous, and teasing, but I'm usually caught off guard when he's teasing."

Her father smiled. "That must be the English in you."

"I guess. But, most important, Chuck is a sincere Christian who shares my goals in life."

He was thoughtful. "I'm sure you will be very happy. Now, will I have the honor of giving the bride away?"

Jonie looked startled. Such an idea had never crossed her mind. She looked at him across the table with a wide-eyed, steady gaze. Finally, she answered his question. "I am sorry if this hurts you. But I believe that the man who has given me a Christian home, a Christian education, and who has assisted my mother through the years in rearing me is entitled to that privilege. I wouldn't think of disappointing him now."

It was her father's turn to sit quietly, studying her. Presently he snubbed out his cigarette and said, "It is only right that he should be the one. I wish you every happiness, Jonie."

Adventure in Nursing

HEALTH PRINCIPLES class was not one of Jonie's favorites. Miss Mazie was interesting if you were interested, but Jonie was not. Not today, anyway. With two weeks of school left, her mind was full of other things.

The voice in front of the blackboard droned on. Across the classroom, pencils and pens raced as copious notes were being taken before final exams.

Jonie's pen lay on the floor. This lecture was the last thing she cared to regiment her mind to. The windows were wide open, and she felt like shouting, "Hey, look, everybody. Don't you know it's spring?"

Suddenly, her mind snapped back into position as the professor's words caught her attention.

"And you young women should frequently examine your breasts for any unusual lumps."

That was something that had never occurred to her before. She gave it momentary consideration before drifting back to summer plans—mostly wedding plans.

After class Jonie hurried to the dormitory to change clothes before dinner and work. The professor's words flashed into her mind again. Hastily she slipped two fingers up under her bra and, for a second, froze as she discovered a pea-sized lump.

"Now, wait a minute," her inner self rationalized. "I'm just imagining because of what I heard." Quickly, she dressed and went to dinner, deciding to forget the incident.

Those last two fleeting weeks of school were crammed with study and tests and term papers. Then, once again, Jonie was chatting with her mother in the familiar pink-and-white bedroom while unpacking and settling in for the few days she had free before going on to a new job. Snatching up a towel, she headed for the shower.

"Hey, Mother, I've got a small lump in my breast," she called casually over her shoulder.

"You have?" Instantly, Donna Owens was on her feet and following her daughter into the bathroom. She placed her cool fingers against the warm flesh, and her eyes widened. "Why, that's about the size of a marble. You're going to see a doctor."

"Oh, Mother! It doesn't hurt."

"Well, it may be nothing to worry about, but it should be checked." She went immediately to the telephone and made the dreaded appointment with a physician whose office was a short distance from Jonie's new job.

A week later Jonie was sitting impatiently in the waiting room when the nurse announced that, as the result of an emergency, the doctor would not be seeing any more patients. Relieved, Jonie returned to the hospital for the classwork she was taking.

At Portland Adventist Hospital Jonie was assigned to a wing on the third floor. "Darcy!" she exclaimed, delighted at meeting her old friend from academy, "what are you doing here?"

"Are you working here, too?" Darcy was equally pleased to renew the friendship. The two girls were laughing and embracing in front of the nurses' desk.

"I took that short training they give for nursing assistants so I could get a summer job," Jonie explained.

"Me too, a year ago," Darcy said, "but summer stretched into winter and winter into another summer. I still want to go to college and take nurse's training, but helping my sis and little brother with their education seems pretty important for right now, anyway."

The head nurse assigned several patients to each girl, and they went off to take temperatures. Jonie's first patient was a doctor and the new nursing assistant felt suddenly inadequate. As the woman opened her mouth to receive the thermometer Jonie dropped it on the floor. She picked up the pieces and realized her hands were shaking. Her next patient was to be given an enema. When she entered the room with the equipment and greeted the woman pleasantly, the grumpy response was, "You're new here."

"That's right."

"Well, you ain't usin' me for no guinea pig." Mrs. Dample's loud voice rang down the corridor. The head nurse hurried into the room, reassured the woman, and sent Zelma, a more experienced aide, to assist Jonie.

The morning couldn't have passed fast enough. Zelma was a large girl with an authoritative air. She didn't help Jonie's confidence very much. At lunch Darcy sympathized and soon had Jonie laughing as she recalled the adventure of her own first day on the floor a year ago. She assured Jonie the afternoon would go better, and she was right.

Each day was filled with new challenges, and Jonie learned to love her work. After the first week Mrs. Dample was completely won over and greeted Jonie's smile with, "Good mornin', Sunshine! You sure are a pleasant sight after that old battle-ax on the night shift.

You're welcome as the flowers in spring."

"Why, Mrs. Dample!" Jonie laughed and went over to pull the drapes. Looking down, she was astonished to see Darren just under the window. She leaned out and spoke his name.

He looked up, as surprised as she had been. "Are you working here, Jonie?"

"That's right."

"So am I. What time do you go to lunch?"

"Twelve-fifteen," she answered.

"See you there?" he questioned.

"Sure!" She flashed that familiar smile.

At noon Darren watched approvingly as Jonie entered the dining room. This was a different Jonie from the one who had assisted him the summer before on the bakery routes. A year of college had given her a bit of assurance. The pounds she had gained were becomingly in the right places, and she had the air of someone who knew where she was going.

He walked toward her. "Well, Nurse Owens, that uniform very nicely helps you to look your role."

"Thank you. It's such a pleasant coincidence to find you working here. I wondered what happened to you after last summer."

"I barely made it for college registration, had to make an emergency trip back home, and later took a job here. I've had a growing interest in hospital chaplaincy."

"Why, Darren, you'll be perfect! When did you decide?"

"I guess it's really as the result of a long illness my mother suffered. When she was hospitalized just after college began last year and I took time out to be with her, I got the exposure that convinced me this is the calling that I'd like to follow."

They continued visiting over their trays, and when they were finished Jonie left with the comfortable feeling about the future of another friend.

On the third floor a number of orthopedic pediatric cases had been brought in. Jonie's heart went out to those children who were confined to wheelchairs or had to spend time in traction. Zelma had the care of four of them. Two were added to Jonie's list of patients.

Zelma was giving 5-year-old Kathy her vitamins when Jonie stood in the doorway to ask a question. The child put the pill in her mouth obediently and watched the two young women in discussion. As Jonie walked away a feeling came over her that the pill had not been swallowed. Jonie stopped. *But why would she hold it in her mouth? I must be mistaken.*

Zelma was ill the following day, and Kathy was in Jonie's care. When the medicine was distributed, Jonie handed Kathy a drink of water. Hardly a spoonful was swallowed. After a moment, Jonie said, "Open up, Kathy." Looking in the child's mouth, she found the tablet. On an impulse, Jonie lifted the edge of the mattress and discovered a good quantity of pink, yellow, and green tablets tucked away. Alarmed at what had happened, Jonie went immediately to her supervisor and asked permission to crush Kathy's prescription into the milkshake she got in the afternoon.

"You certainly may," the woman responded. "Too bad this wasn't done sooner."

"I wonder," Jonie said thoughtfully, "if it wouldn't be easier to keep an eye on all these children if they were in that one large ward at the end of the hall."

"I believe you have a point," said the nurse. "We've sure had more youngsters with broken bones this vacation than usual, and they are a handful."

When Zelma returned she was put to work moving

beds with adult patients from the large ward to several
smaller ones. At dinnertime, she announced that, with
the influx of pediatric patients, she would soon be very
busy with the little rascals down at her end of the wing
in the new children's ward.

A wistful feeling swept over Jonie. That ward could
be so much fun, she thought.

The afternoon shift finished the transfer, and when
Jonie arrived the following morning she was delighted
to find she had been assigned to the pediatric ward.

It was a full morning of temperatures, bedpans,
baths, and bedmaking. Jonie was busy telling stories,
had the children singing rounds, and was glad for the
heavy closed door to confine the noise to their area. After
lunch she gave them twenty minutes for a pillow fight
before settling them down for naps. Then she quietly
tidied the room for the next shift.

"How'd it go?" Darcy asked as they signed out.

"Oh, Darcy, I loved it!" Jonie enthused, though a bit
tired.

When 10-year-old Matthew, who was in traction,
confided in Jonie that he didn't like the night nurse and
he bet he could scare the socks off her, Jonie assisted
him in stringing up a soft gray catnip mouse to pull
across her path in the night. It had the desired effect, to
his satisfaction. Luckily, the door was shut about
midnight when the woman let out a sudden shriek.

Zelma walked into the ward one afternoon just as
Jonie finished a story at naptime. "I've been told to
watch the kids. Miss Davis wants you."

Jonie hurried to the main desk, a little concerned.

"Miss Owens, would you take a few moments and
check Mrs. Dample out? She particularly asked for you."

"Certainly," Jonie said, feeling relieved. "I was
afraid you were giving me a new assignment. I mean a

steady one. I wouldn't like that."

"You really like your work in peds, don't you?"

"Very much," Jonie said smiling. "Almost, it tempts me to take up nursing as a vocation."

Mrs. Dample was dressed to leave. Jonie helped her into a wheelchair and arranged her suitcase and a potted plant. They checked out and got on the elevator to go to a lower level, where a taxi was waiting. "This hospital is certainly changing, with all the remodeling and the new wing being built," the woman remarked.

Jonie agreed as she pushed the button for the lower floor. The elevator hummed, and suddenly the feeling of suspension changed to a fast drop. The fall ended in a hard jolt. They were on the ground a few feet below the bottom floor level.

"Are you all right, Mrs. Dample?"

"I'm fine. This here wheelchair's got good springs. That was some fast ride!"

Jonie couldn't get the elevator back to the proper level. She pounded on the door and was rescued by some workmen who assisted her from the outside of the electric prison. Jonie winced as she took the wheelchair out a side entrance and up the hill to the taxi. Her back felt wrenched.

"Oh, I almost forgot to give you this," Mrs. Dample said. She opened her purse and took out a gift-wrapped package. "That's for the wedding, dear."

"Why, thank you, Mrs. Dample!" Jonie smiled her pleasure. "And after you were my first guinea pig!" The woman chuckled and patted the girl's arm.

"I appreciated your sunshine, dear. Have a happy married life."

Jonie was glad she had the next two days off. The fall and the nerve strain left her a little stiff.

A Wedding or Not?

THE SUMMER flew, filled with work and those too-few happy occasions when Chuck arrived to share in the numerous activities that brides become involved in. Caught up in the excitement, Jonie gave little heed to the growing lump within her breast. Occasionally, when reaching over her head, a slight tenderness annoyed her as the lower band of her bra pulled up and tightened against her flesh.

Jonie had a difficult time settling her mind about attendants. "I love all my friends so much, I hate to leave anyone out," she told Chuck.

"But, honey, if you are paying for most of this yourself, how can you afford flowers for more than two or three girls?"

Jonie considered his question a moment. Then, beaming, she hopped up, singing, "I've got it! I've got it! I've got it!"

"Got what?" Chuck laughed at her antics.

"Today I bought fourteen candles—tall, pale, creamy yellow tapers."

"Yes, for the candelabra," he added.

"That's right! So I will put lace frills around the bottom of each with long narrow ribbons trailing. I will get a bolt of pale yellow taffeta and cut off pieces for each girl to make a dress and have two groups of seven girls carry the candles from the tallest down to the shortest on each side, like a candelabra."

"You mean a *humalabra,*" he corrected. "I've never heard of it before."

"No matter. You probably just coined a new word."

"I have to make up new words to keep up with your ideas," he stated drily. "Now what about the cake?"

"You would think of that, and it's all taken care of. The bakery where I worked a year ago is giving us a beautiful large, tiered cake. Isn't that terrific? Only let's hope the guys in the back shop don't put some tricks in it. And, Chuck, the hospital is helping me with the punch. They let me have it wholesale. Lucky for us your father is a commercial printer and photographer. That took care of the announcements and photos, the best ever."

"And I've been worrying for you!"

"But that's not all, Chuck. No one would ever believe what a dream of a wedding gown I've purchased for next to nothing. It's a rich white satin, but the lace in the neck was utterly ruined. Someone tried it on and got lipstick all over it. Mother is replacing it with exquisite new lace, and I'm sewing tiny seed pearls on it. What a job, but I had planned to make the whole thing, and this is ever so much easier."

"When do I get a sneak preview?"

"You won't, if I can help it!"

He was amused at her quick answer.

"So what else are you doing with your spare time?"

"Canning, of course. Can't forget the long winters and keeping you fed properly. I picked wild blackberries one day after work and put them up for pies. When I think of berry pies it reminds me of—— Chuck, I know where we can get our flowers!" Jonie suddenly changed subjects. "Can you take me for a ride?"

"Sure. Anywhere you want to go."

Several miles into the country, they stopped at a tiny shack surrounded by open fields of beautiful gladioluses. Row upon row of color captured their attention.

Jonie hurried down the path and up onto the frail-looking porch. Chuck, watching from the car, smiled to himself. A bent, elderly man opened to the eager knock. He wore faded striped bib overalls and looked as though he lived outdoors.

"Mr. Yancy, do you remember me?"

He chuckled. "Sure I do. You are the berry-pie girl. I haven't seen you for a long time. Still peddling?"

"No, I'm not peddling bakery goods this year. I'm getting married in a couple of weeks and I want to know what you do with all those beautiful flowers before you harvest the bulbs."

"Not very much. You need some glads?"

"I'll make you a deal. Supposing I bake you some bread, cookies, pies, and cake. You've got that little freezer out back, and I remember your sweet tooth."

"Say, now you have got a deal. Will they be as good as the day-olds you saved for me from the peddlin' truck last summer?"

Chuck leaned out the car window. "Lots better than that, sir. I can vouch for it."

"Oh, you must be the one marrying this cook!"

"You betcha," Chuck answered, grinning with pride.

"Congratulations. You two come pick all the flowers you want when you're ready."

They drove back to town, where Jonie put Chuck to work cracking nuts for brownies while she began making bread.

Jonie went to the ranch to be with Chuck and his family for her weekend off work. Sharing a room with his little sister, she was dimly aware of the sound of an engine outside the window early Sunday morning. Pulling the pillow over her head, she snuggled deeper into sleep and somewhere in the distance it seemed she could hear someone calling her.

Beyond the back door, Chuck was tilling the ground for his mother, who watched with interest from the kitchen window. He raised his hand to wave to her and at that moment the tiller hit a rock, caught his pants, and dug into the flesh of his left leg. Blood spurted, and it was then that Jonie heard her name being called frantically from the kitchen.

The girl jumped out of bed, threw a blanket over her nightgown, and raced for the kitchen. She followed the screaming woman out the door to where Chuck was lying on the ground. His leg was badly chewed, and he was obviously in shock.

They were soon speeding to the clinic while Chuck's little sister remained behind to phone the doctor. After a quick inspection of the injury, he informed Jonie that she would have to do for an assistant. "This is going to take a lot of sutures," he announced briskly.

When Chuck, pale and tired, went home again, fifty-three stitches were laced into his leg, and he would not be walking for a while.

Jonie picked the beautiful gladioluses alone and felt fortunate that, even though Chuck was limping, he was back on his feet for the wedding. On that afternoon pale delicate flowers in their white wicker baskets stood at the ends of the long green-carpeted aisle of the Columbia Academy church.

An hour before the ceremony Jonie sat a bit tensely in the old-fashioned bathtub at Aunt Nelly's house, where she had spent so many hours with Carol their senior year in academy. Surrounded by bubbles, she was trying to relax for a few moments before putting on her wedding dress. She leaned back and closed her eyes. In the distance she could hear cars already arriving at the church across the street. Panic of a type she had never before known gripped her. She wanted to leap out of the tub, grab her clothes, and run as far and as fast as she could.

"What am I doing? Oh, what am I doing?" Rinsing off the bubbles, she toweled and dressed hurriedly. "I can't go through with it. Oh, Father, what is wrong with me? You have given me the precious love of a wonderful man. Why all these last-minute doubts? Why am I so scared?"

Like calm after a tempest came peace following the panic. Jonie relaxed, confident that her loving Father had chosen wisely for her.

With her hair in rollers and her wedding gown over her arm, she hurried to the church. As she ducked in the side door someone on the wide steps spotted her and remarked, "There goes the bride now, so I guess we aren't late. She's certainly not ready."

In the cool, dim lower regions of the large church, Jonie met her waiting attendants, who took over the final dressing of the bride. The girls rejoiced in their efforts and in a few minutes a beautifully gowned and well-groomed Jonie repaired to the mothers' room in the upper hallway to wait for Mr. Owens.

Meanwhile, the pastor's study was a scene of amusement and perplexity. Chuck stood leaning on his temporary crutch when Jonie's brother, Jimmy, the best man, came limping in.

"What happened to you?" Chuck wanted to know.

"I was working on my car when another car close beside it rolled, and my leg got caught between the two. It's nothing too serious." He raised his pant leg to show a badly discolored, bruised calf.

Chuck whistled. "My buddy, who's also standing with us, just had an operation on his knee. At least Gale won't be limping."

But when Gale arrived he was wearing a walking cast. The three incredulous young men gathered about him with the same question, "You too?"

He flashed his ready smile. "Afraid so. I put an ax through my foot while working in the woods."

"Oh, no," Jimmy groaned. "What'll we do if Sis faints?"

"Faints!" they all echoed.

"Yes, Jonie always faints when she's scared."

Gale looked around at his friends, all leaning on crutches. He took a coin from his pocket dramatically. "Heads or tails—on who's picking her up."

"Don't worry. Jonie's not fainting. Jimmy's pulling our other legs," Chuck assured them. They laughed with relief as Columbia Academy's principal, Mr. Kent, came through the door ready to take his place on the platform.

From the mothers' room Jonie watched with pride and amusement as the young men who had left their crutches at the pastor's study door hobbled out front.

The pale golden "humalabra" of girls surrounded them, and the candles were lighted. Before the two bridesmaids walked up the aisle, Linda gave Jonie a quick hug, and Jonie passed it on to Chuck's little sister, who suddenly looked quite grown-up in her long maid-of-honor dress and wide-brimmed hat.

"Do I stand by my daddy?" the flower girl asked, pointing a small finger to her father, who was holding his Bible on the platform.

"Yes, dear, right by your daddy. Oh," Jonie exclaimed, "where is *my* father?" She looked into the hall and entry. "He's not here! I saw Mother go in. What has happened?" She was alarmed. "Susie, go slow. Go real slow."

On a back country road Mr. Owens was frantically trying to find his way. "How could I have gotten lost?" he muttered. I should know these roads. I went to school out here. Never had a car in those days, though. Why did I think I could find anything open today, anyway? I could have just knotted my broken shoestring. I can't let Jonie down." He spun to a stop and rolled down the window.

"Say, there, sir," he waved. The man picking apples got down from his ladder and walked slowly to the fence. "Can you tell me how to find Columbia Academy?"

"Sure can," came the answer.

With the directions in mind, Mr. Owens sped the last few miles as the flower girl scattered her petals down the long aisle and smiled up at her daddy, who reached out to her.

There was a pause. The bells sounded clearly now. The organ began pealing forth the bride's entrance, and the congregation waited. One by one they looked back at the empty doorway. Jonie stood hidden in the shadows, nervously biting her lip. The organist played a bit louder. "She's fainted," Jimmy whispered, and Chuck turned white.

I'll just have to go it alone, Jonie thought. She stepped across the foyer, falling in step with the rhythm of the march. *Heavenly Father, thank You that I never have to really walk alone.*

A hurried rustle beside her brought a radiant smile to the face of the bride as Mr. Owens took her arm and they entered the door together.

Wonders Never Cease

"LOOK AT the horizon, Chuck, it's like my love."

"I've no doubt you can explain that if I ask," he said.

"Are you asking?" she questioned.

"Of course, Mrs. Richards," he smiled teasingly at her.

She pointed seaward and said, "My love is like that blue, blue ribbon, a length of sky and ocean blended. Mists drawn above return to the sea. Each without the other would cease to be." She looked back at him.

"Those were words worthy of a framework of music," he said softly.

The hour was late, but the strip of coastal highway gleamed in the moonlight as the soft chuckle of waves was heard on the pebbles at low tide. The young honeymooners began reminiscing about the scenes of the afternoon.

"Remember when we knelt to pray and Gale sang 'The Lord's Prayer,' then Susie escaped her father's grasp and pushed those buttons that rang all the Sabbath school chimes," Jonie asked.

"So that is what happened!" Chuck exclaimed. "I thought you had planned it."

"No, it was just a beautiful accident," Jonie said.

"Wasn't that something! I'll never forget all those

fellows with their cars lined up facing the campus and how we fled out the back door of the girls' dorm and onto the side road that Mr. Kent and Mr. Corning had blocked with that car. Those guys worked like mad to shove it in the ditch while we were fleeing down the road with no lights till we turned the corner. Good thing we had friends who knew the perfect getaway." Chuck laughed in remembrance of their successful escape.

"And I'll never forget my dear dean who was helping me out of my wedding gown when you popped into the room. She looked at me in my slip and at you with such disapproval. You were shouting, 'Hurry up, Jonie! Will you?' She grabbed up my suit and held it in front of me. I was racing into my blouse to take off for the chase and she was determined to protect my modesty. Then she said, 'Oh, I forgot, he is your husband.'" Peals of laughter were carried on the salt breeze.

"Look, Chuck! Look at the cottage over there. See it?"

Chuck slowed the car. "I don't believe it!"

"Believe it, believe it, honey. It's real or the moonlight is deceiving us."

They turned in the long drive and parked in front of several small cottages. The last one facing the ocean was gray with pink flower boxes and pink wooden lawn furniture on the grass in front.

They both got out of the car and went to the manager's cottage. Chuck tapped lightly. The lights were out inside. Jonie tapped a second time with urgency, and a gentleman in a bathrobe answered. He looked at them from behind the window glass and shook his head No.

"Please, sir, couldn't we rent that cabin at the end?" Chuck asked loudly.

The man hesitated and in the pause that ensued

Jonie added, "It's our honeymoon."

The man smiled and opened the door. "Here's the key. Honeymooners get special out-of-season discounts and special rates by the week. You want to inspect it?"

"It's quite all right," they both said. They walked down the path in the moonlight. It was just as they had dreamed.

They returned sunburned and freckled from the coast trip to try to pack all their gifts and belongings into the small mobile home they had purchased and had left parked on the ranch.

Chuck was a big hero in a farming community of many small boys. He often umpired their baseball games in the evening after work, but the last few days left before returning to college were spent on the ranch preparing to leave. Jonie continued working, canning, and answering the door to a parade of young boys who curiously looked her over and timidly inquired whether Chuck could come out and play. Some of these same youngsters, not-so-timidly asked Chuck whether Jonie knew how to bake cookies.

Back at college, Jonie was busy with those first groceries to buy, meals to cook, summer's canned fruit to proudly serve, classes to attend, her little mobile home to keep tidy, and a husband to love.

Then the anxiety about the growing lump in her breast began to occupy her mind as she tried to study. It was now the size of a walnut and could no longer be ignored.

Gathering her close in his arms one night, Chuck said, "Honey, I talked to a doctor about you today. He wants you to come in tomorrow. OK?"

Against his shoulder, she nodded in the darkness, fearful of the outcome.

Her natural shyness did not escape the doctor and
aroused his sympathy. He gently told her that surgery
might be necessary; however, he would like to observe
the lump for two weeks and see if, by chance, it would
disappear with her monthly cycle. Jonie knew it would
not. She had lived with it constantly for more than eight
months. Surgery was inevitable and her heart ached
with fear.

It was autumn Religious Emphasis Week on campus, a quiet time of sharing God's love. The speaker
encouraged personal testimonies, and Jonie listened
one evening as Stan told of a miraculous healing in his
life. He closed, expressing his faith in prayer. Jonie was
drawn to her feet and found herself moving to the front
of the auditorium where, trembling, she took the
microphone. Before that sea of faces, she said shyly, "I
have a small lump. The doctor says it should be
removed by surgery next week. I too am sure that by
faith, and with your prayers and mine, I can be healed.
Please pray for me."

What she expected, she wasn't sure—perhaps a slow
dissolvement the same way it had grown. But nothing
happened. Each night in Chuck's arms she pleaded with
the Almighty. "Please, Father, don't let this happen to
me." She was not aware that the women and men in the
dormitory clubs made it a matter of prayer that week
also.

A fire drill emptied the classrooms onto the frosty
November campus. Amidst the noise and student
laughter, Stan, whose testimony had inspired Jonie,
walked up and greeted her with, "How are you doing?"

"Fine," she smiled back.

"But, how are you *really?*" His serious gaze held her
eyes.

"Oh," she instantly sobered, "do you mean, is it still there?"

He nodded.

"Yes, it is," she hesitantly replied.

Sternly, he said, "Jonie, if you pray with faith, God can heal you."

"I know," she said quietly.

"Then, *have faith.*" He walked away, and Jonie stood in the chilled sunshine, her faith challenged.

She met Chuck at the post office, and they walked toward their mobile home together. He was glancing through the mail. Jonie was preoccupied with her thoughts.

"But, Father," she said, staring at the cracks in the sidewalk, "I know You can heal me. If it be Your will, *heal me.*"

They entered their small home, and Jonie hurried to change clothes before getting lunch. As had become a habit, she slipped her fingers up under her bra. For a moment she stood motionless, then screamed, "Honey, come quick!"

Alarmed, Chuck ran to the bedroom. Jonie's face was radiant with relief. "Honey, it has happened! The lump is gone! I'm healed!"

They cried in each others' arms as they knelt to thank God.

Disrupted Plans

AUTUMN TURNED to winter, and Jonie's heart sang with gladness and the wonder of love from both above and within her small home. Debby, a classmate from academy, lived nearby and shared the birth of her little girl, Donna Jo.

"This child has a great heritage," Jonie said to the happy mother, only half teasing. "After all, her mom was valedictorian of our class, and her father was an illustrious Columbia Academy Student Body president."

Work was scarce in the college area, so Chuck and one of his married friends traveled over the icy hills to Pendleton, Oregon, to jobs at the Harris Pine Mills, from which they returned at two in the morning. It was a hard grind, but Chuck did not complain.

Gail was back in college and steadily dating Ted. Knowing Jonie's passion for ice-skating and hockey, they often stopped by the trailer house on cold clear nights to take her with them to the frozen pond. On one such night they returned to find the small oil heater wasn't working. Ted checked it over and decided the lines were frozen. He poured a bit of oil inside the fire box and said, "Now I'll light a small fire that will clear the lines and get it going again." He threw in a match and a loud whoosh took the flames right up the wall. Gail jumped back in horror as Ted, using his good left arm, whipped at the fire with a small rug, trying to smother the bright tongues of flame traveling across the wooden ceiling. Jonie dashed out the door to yank loose the oil tank that was attached to the side of the trailer before it ignited. The fire burned out quickly and three shivering young people huddled under the blankets until Chuck arrived. Gail dozed while Ted and Jonie talked on and on, too wound up to sleep.

Jonie often stayed awake to study until Chuck was safely back home from his treacherous trip through sleet or snow. The mobile home court was new, and the Richards' trailer was the only occupant besides the manager's. Rain falling on snowdrifts laid a freezing, icy crust across the vacant area surrounding the trailer. One night as Jonie sat on the bed and leaned against the back wall beside the window studying, the sound of approaching footsteps brought her suddenly alert.

Outside, the manager's small, yippy dog ran bouncing and yapping toward the trailer as a hand shoved hard against the window, then hurled something at the dog. Jonie was motionless with fright. The dog retreated briefly and the window was tried again. Then the manager's light went on and Jonie heard heavy boots breaking ice as the intruder ran.

The next morning the manager told Chuck that he had opened his door in time to see his dog leaping fiercely at a man climbing over the fence. Chuck hugged Jonie and said, "Remind me never to complain about yippy little pipsqueaks again. The manager is putting in night lights. He and his wife were really frightened for you. So am I," he breathed, hugging her again.

Christmas brought a bit of overspending on Christmas gifts for loved ones and then a few hungry days when the groceries didn't stretch far enough. January rolled around with Chuck giving his creative assistance to Jonie's pet projects. She was involved in the American Temperance Society and served as secretary of the college chapter. Merlin Kretschmar, the president, was energetic and ambitious in the promotion of their combined ideas. Over sandwiches and salad in the little mobile home or a lovely meal in Dr. Kretschmar's home, they planned and put into motion the activities planned for the Temperance Fair that spring.

Then the fateful letter arrived. Chuck's father was to have surgery for possible cancer. After an anxious time at home, they were relieved to know that Mr. Richards was on the mend, and they prayed that he be spared many more years.

Another letter that was dreaded, yet half expected, arrived from Uncle Sam. Chuck was to report for his physical for the United States Army. The two young folks moved their mobile home back to the ranch and waited for the induction.

"Wherever you go, I'm going, too," Jonie said firmly.

"No, you don't! The Army's no place for women!"

"Then how come so many join up or follow?"

"That's not for my wife!" Chuck exploded, unhappy with the latest developments in his life. "The Army is for GI Joes. Period."

His wife smiled a wry little smile of determination. "So, just meet Mrs. GI Jonie."

And Chuck knew she meant it.